GCHQ

PUZZLES
FOR
SPIES

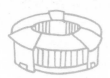

PUZZLES
FOR
SPIES

GCHQ

PUFFIN

PUFFIN BOOKS

UK | USA | Canada | Ireland | Australia
India | New Zealand | South Africa

Puffin Books is part of the Penguin Random House group of companies
whose addresses can be found at global.penguinrandomhouse.com.
www.penguin.co.uk   www.puffin.co.uk   www.ladybird.co.uk

First published 2022

001

Text copyright © Crown Copyright, 2022
Illustration copyright © Shutterstock, 2022
Photos © Crown Copyright, by kind permission of Director GCHQ

With additional thanks to Bletchley Park

The moral right of the author and illustrator has been asserted

Proceeds from GCHQ's share of the Advance and Royalties for this book, estimated in the first
year to be £20,000, will go to The Royal Foundation of The Duke and Duchess of Cambridge
(registered charity number: 1132048). To date, GCHQ Puzzle Books I and II have
raised over £600,000 for the charity's work on mental health.

Interior design by Dynamo Ltd
Printed and bound in Great Britain by Clays Ltd, Elcograf S.p.A.

The authorized representative in the EEA is Penguin Random House Ireland,
Morrison Chambers, 32 Nassau Street, Dublin D02 YH68
A CIP catalogue record for this book is available from the British Library

ISBN: 978–0–241–57990–9

All correspondence to:
Puffin Books, Penguin Random House Children's
One Embassy Gardens, 8 Viaduct Gardens
London SW11 7BW

To the hard-working people of GCHQ –
past, present and future.

CONTENTS

The Royal Foundation of The Duke and Duchess of Cambridge

The Royal Foundation of The Duke and Duchess of Cambridge mobilises leaders, businesses and people so that together we can address society's greatest challenges.

Encouraging people to speak about and seek support with their mental health has been an important part of our work since The Duke and Duchess of Cambridge led the nation's biggest ever conversation on mental health with the Heads Together campaign in 2017.

We have continued this work ever since, with vital services and resources supporting communities from early childhood to adulthood, front-line responders to football fans, teenagers to teachers. While the conversation is changing on this important issue, there is more work to be done.

The Royal Foundation will continue to build awareness of the importance of establishing the core mental health foundations that allow us to go on to thrive as individuals, with one another, as a community and as a society. Thank you for supporting the development and delivery of this vital work.

We are delighted that the brilliant minds at GCHQ have been busy working on a third puzzle book, and that this edition is designed for younger readers. Hopefully this might mean we find them easier to solve...!

As a family, we are no strangers to the vital work of GCHQ. We have seen first-hand how staff constantly adapt to face new threats, and we remain inspired by how committed staff are to protecting our national security.

The COVID-19 pandemic presented one of the biggest global challenges in recent history. It impacted our ability to go to work, to school, and to socialise in the way we are all accustomed to. This affected every one of us and sadly we know the true scale of the pandemic's impact on the nation's mental health will not be fully understood for years to come.

Your support through the purchase of the book will ensure that The Royal Foundation is able to continue its mental health work at a time when that support is needed more than ever before.

We look forward to helping our children solve these puzzles, and hope that this book brings friends and families together to start rich conversations. Talking openly about mental health can be the first step in removing stigma, fear and isolation. Just like at GCHQ, bringing different perspectives together can often be the key to unlocking a solution you can't quite find on your own.

Good luck to everyone!

Foreword by Director GCHQ

This is GCHQ's third puzzle book. In our first two editions we shared our passion for puzzling while also raising vital money to support mental health charities. Having thoroughly baffled the grown-ups, we thought we'd write this book especially for children. Don't let that fool you though – it doesn't mean we've made things easy! It wouldn't be a GCHQ puzzle book if it didn't have you scratching your head, but that's all part of the fun.

GCHQ's mission is to help keep the country safe. We've been doing that for over one hundred years. Through our understanding of communications technology (like telephones, computers and the internet), we protect the UK from threats – everything from cyber attacks to terrorist attacks in the real world. Some of our work has to stay secret so that we keep our advantage over those who are trying to do bad things. But I will share one thing with you: it is the amazing people who come to work for us that make GCHQ brilliant.

Puzzling is a form of problem solving; it helps to get you thinking in different ways. But it is a myth that everyone at GCHQ is great at puzzles. We are all different – and that is our great strength. People come to work for us from across the country, from all sorts of backgrounds. They work together, each offering their own perspective and way of thinking to solve difficult problems. The thing we all have in common is commitment to the security of the nation. I am incredibly proud of everyone at GCHQ and what they achieve together to protect our country.

While problem solving exercises our brains, it is equally important to take care of our minds. Our first two books raised a staggering amount of money for mental health charities and enabled them to do valuable work in communities across the country. I'm delighted that through this book we will continue supporting this cause. Our profits from sales will be donated to the Royal Foundation of The Duke and Duchess of Cambridge.

The work of Their Royal Highnesses has helped many people – including children – be more open about mental health. I want to thank them for both their patronage of this cause and their support to GCHQ. And thanks to the teams from across GCHQ who worked to create this book and whose incredible talent is evident in every page. I can't name them, but they know who they are.

As you embark on your not-so-secret mission of working through this book, you'll encounter a range of different types of puzzles in each section that all require different approaches. If you're struggling, don't give up. Nobody is good at all types of puzzles. Perhaps your talent will shine in another chapter.

Good luck!

Sir Jeremy Fleming
Director GCHQ

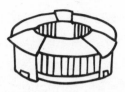

An Introduction to GCHQ

We are the Government Communications Headquarters, more commonly known as GCHQ.

We are an intelligence, security and cyber agency. Put simply, our mission is to keep the United Kingdom safe. And we've been doing this for many years.

GCHQ was formed over one hundred years ago, shortly after the end of the First World War. We are a top secret organisation, so when we first started out only a handful of people knew that we even existed. Today, we're able to tell people a bit more about what we do.

We focus on communications – so information shared between people, organisations and countries – to identify and help stop dangers that the United Kingdom might face. We work closely with the two other intelligence agencies in the United Kingdom, MI5 and MI6. Often the same threat is faced by different countries, so we also work with other agencies around the world.

People sometimes refer to us as spies, but we're much more than that. We're analysts, linguists, engineers, mathematicians, programmers, codebreakers (and that's just the start!) – all working together in brilliant teams to solve seemingly impossible problems. (And if some of those jobs aren't familiar to you, don't worry – they will be once you've finished this book.)

We also work with the police to help them tackle serious crime. We support the military when they are deployed in conflict. Through our National Cyber Security Centre (or NCSC), we help make the country the safest place to live and work online, tackling the dangers that might affect you, your friends and family in cyberspace. In 2020, we played a big part in protecting the NHS during the Covid-19 pandemic.

New technology allows people around the world to share information and talk to each other like never before. Back when we began, phones were rare. Now over 75% of the world has access to a smartphone! That's changed the type of threats we continue to protect everyone from.

We have to be creative, fast-thinking and prepared to work with the most amazing new technology. That could be some clever new computer coding that we put together, or a new machine we need to build, to help us break a code or solve a problem.

The people at GCHQ come from a range of backgrounds. Some join straight from school, others come to us from a totally different job. There is no one journey to GCHQ. One thing everyone has in common is that they have the potential to learn new things, and want a job that helps to keep the country – and the world – safe.

In this book, you'll find out about our top secret work, and discover the incredible story of GCHQ: from breaking the Enigma code at the famous Bletchley Park to how we spread across the country, with different offices up and down the UK – one of which is our doughnut-shaped headquarters in Cheltenham (commonly known as the Doughnut) and our new office in the heart of the city of Manchester.

Scarborough

Manchester

Cheltenham   London

Bude

Because so much of what we do involves solving tough problems, we love puzzles. Many of us even create puzzles for fun in our spare time. We've already published some of these in two GCHQ puzzle books, which we hope you might find on your nearest bookshelf! This book, however, is for **you** – the problem solvers of the future.

Each chapter has challenges from the different areas of work at GCHQ, so you can get a real sense of what we actually do! There are codes to break, languages to learn, brainteasers to solve and even some robots to build. We hope some or all of these chapters might spark an interest in subjects you may have never thought about. Who knows what hidden talents you might discover . . . and what it might mean for the future.

We hope you enjoy it.

YOUR MISSION BRIEFING

Dear Puzzlers,

You don't have to be a quiz champion – or even top of the class – to work at GCHQ. You just need to have an interest in figuring things out and an infectious curiosity. This is why puzzles are so important to us.

We don't spend all of our time putting together jigsaws and filling out crosswords – but by creating and solving puzzles, our teams can work on tackling new problems in different and inventive ways. It's also really fun (at least, we think so!).

The thinking and methods that go into puzzles can really help in our important day jobs. Imagine being faced with a tricky problem, or trying to track down that crucial nugget of information (a needle in a haystack!). We approach these in the same way we do a puzzle. We need to think outside the box and practise spotting patterns. All of which gives us a crucial advantage in the work we do.

Your mission – should you choose to accept it – is to navigate your way through the chapters in this book, which are full of fiendish puzzles, brilliant brainteasers and tricky conundrums.

There are eight chapters in total. The first is full of puzzles to get you started, and the ones that follow relate to the different types of work we do at GCHQ. They focus on languages, engineering, codebreaking, analysis, mathematics, coding and cybersecurity. We have lined up eight of our talented GCHQ colleagues to join you as your puzzle host in each area. They will be your expert guides, helping you find your way through.

Because each chapter is focused on a particular type of work we do, you'll find they each have different types of puzzles. Begin each chapter at the start, as this is where your GCHQ host will tell you about their jobs and interests. The puzzles will also get harder as you progress through the chapter. On the way, you will learn about the subject of the chapter and how it is used at GCHQ, and the puzzles will allow you to test your skills in that area. We'll also give you some facts about GCHQ and our exciting history, and our historian David is on hand to tell you a bit about some of the amazing people who have worked here.

Some puzzles may appear tricky at first, but once you get the hang of them, you can learn to spot patterns, think around a problem and apply your mind to finding the solution. In each chapter, your GCHQ host will be ready to help with hints and tips, so don't worry if you get stuck!

You may find it helpful to have a pencil and paper to hand as you aren't required to solve everything in your head. But, in the end, this is your book: make notes, draw doodles and work things out where there's space.

Different chapters will appeal to different people, so if you like one subject in particular then that's the chapter to focus on. As well as the individual chapters there is also a **final Team Challenge**, which requires combining all the different skills. You could get together with your friends or classmates and solve it together – just like a team at GCHQ.

And keep your eyes peeled. Throughout the book there are things hidden – even on the front cover!

We don't expect you to complete every puzzle first time. It's not that kind of book. There are no tests, no revision, no competitions, no prizes (just the satisfaction of solving the puzzle!). We hope you find something here that interests and challenges you. Most importantly, we want you to have fun.

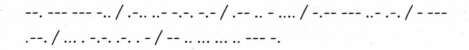

--. --- --- -.. / .-.. ..- -.-. -.- / .-- .. - .... / - .-.. --- ..- .-. / - --- .--. / .... . -.-. .-. . - / -- .. .. --- -.

Chapter One
GETTING STARTED

An introduction to puzzling

Hi puzzlers! My name is Colin. I work in a part of GCHQ called the National Cyber Security Centre (NCSC), but thanks to a passion for puzzling, I've also earned the unofficial title of GCHQ's **Chief Puzzler!**

Solving puzzles is an analytical skill – that means examining something to find out what it is or what makes it work. Analysis is at the heart of much of what we do at GCHQ, which is why puzzling is so important to us here. Maybe you're good at solving puzzles? Even if you don't think you are, as long as you're curious and ready to learn, you can develop the skills you need to be an amazing puzzle solver.

I started my first job at GCHQ over thirty years ago and have since worked in both intelligence and cyber security. When I began my career here, I wanted an interesting job with the

staying safe online

gathering and analysing information

chance to do something important. What I've done at GCHQ over the past three decades has helped to keep the country safe, which is why I've chosen to work here for so long.

When I was at school, I liked maths, numbers and solving puzzles (of course!), and my favourite book growing up was **The Moscow Puzzles**.

My role at the NCSC is all about the future. This means looking into new technologies that are being developed, and ensuring these technologies have security built in **before** they are used by members of the public, like you and your friends, so we can better protect our country and its people.

My favourite thing about working at GCHQ is that so many people, with so many different skills, are working together for one reason: to keep the country and its citizens safe. I also love that there really isn't a typical day here. Each one is different.

Setting puzzles has some great perks. Are you a fan of the TV programme **Blue**

Peter? I was once the Mystery Voice in an episode of the show, which included a visit to the GCHQ Top Secret exhibition at the Science Museum as part of a puzzle competition. So most importantly of all, I have a Blue Peter Badge!

Coming up with ideas for puzzles requires a good imagination – a bit like writing a poem or drawing a picture on a blank piece of paper. It can be a lot of fun! The hardest part of puzzle setting is checking to make sure there aren't any mistakes.

You'll see me pop up again here and there in the chapter to give you clues, and if you get stuck on any questions you'll find me on page 34 along with some hints and tips!

Good luck, and **happy puzzling**!

COLIN

1 The early bird

These animals each have a wrong letter. Can you work out what the correct letters should be, and find the animals? For example, FROM could become FROG.

LEOTARD   **DECK**   **WOLD**

BOX   **PEG**   **SHAKE**

The missing letters reveal a hidden animal. What is it?

2 Cryptic calendar

Which date follows the ones listed below?

7 January,   **8 February,**   **5 March,**

5 April,   **3 May,**   **4 June,**   **_____**

Do you know which country celebrates independence on this date?

3 Food for thought

Hidden in each of these words is something you can eat. Can you find it?

As an example, the word PYJAMAS contains the word JAM.

STEWARD   **OCTONION**

TRICERATOPS   **BUNNY**

BEGGAR   **JUMPSTART**

When you've found them all, the first letters of each food spell out a refreshing dessert – which one?

4 Microdot-to-microdot

Join the dots. Instead of a number, each dot is next to a word. Join two dots if the last letter of one word is the first letter of another. So, for instance, 'thum**b**' should be joined to '**b**anana'.

What is revealed when the dots are joined?

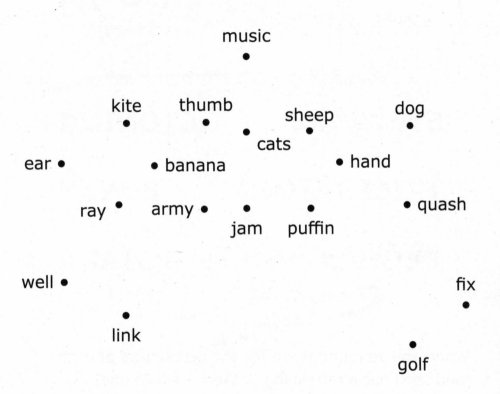

5 Excellent Entertaining Limerick

This puzzle was tough for the setter

Rhyming did not make things better

Our limerick wish

Uncover the fish

Take a good look at each line's first letter

6 Frankenstein's wordsearch

All but one of the rows and columns in this wordsearch contain words that are a part of the human body. Which is the odd row or column out?

T	O	O	F	W	L
E	N	H	R	A	E
L	I	A	T	J	G
B	H	N	O	S	E
O	S	D	E	Y	E
W	Y	M	M	U	T

Some of the words are written backwards or upside down!

7 Mini crossword

Down

1 Curved yellow fruit.

2 Country whose cities include Ottawa and Toronto.

3 A well-known activist who advocates for girls' education, _____ Yousafzai.

Across

4 Swahili phrase meaning 'no worries', Hakuna _____ .

5 Country with a big canal.

6 Large desert in Africa.

8 Fishing expedition

The people below have been busy catching fish.
Can you work out who caught which fish, and
then draw a straight line between the end of their
fishing line and the mouth of the fish it caught?

Then tell us how they all got home.

9 Richard of York

Each of these words are missing some letters.
But each list follows a pattern. What words
would you add to make the lists complete?

a) ED, _____, ELLOW, REEN,
    LUE, NDIGO, IOLET

b) ERCUR, ENU, _____, AR,
    UPITE, ATUR, RANU, EPTUN

The letters are in a different order for this
last one, so it's a little harder!

c) NOM, EUT, _____,
    UHT, IRF, TAS, NUS

10 Burn me

All of the words below are (anagrams) –
unscramble them and then work out what
order they should go in. In this order,
which is first and which is last?

An anagram is a new word or phrase created using exactly the same letters of another word or phrase but in a different order.

HERD UNDONE

HIT ENTER

IFFY TETHER

THY TWEETING

TIN YEN

TWIX TOYS

TYNE ROOF

WITTY THOR

YES VENT

YOU FIGHTER

Check the hint on page 36 if you get stuck!

Hello puzzlers, I'm Dr David Abrutat, the GCHQ Historian. It's my job to tell the world about our fascinating history. I get to explore our vast archives, where we have some incredible documents and artefacts, from codebreaking machines to top secret telephones. It helps me to piece together our past.

As you go through the book, I'll be telling you a little bit more about the history of GCHQ and showing you some of those ingenious artefacts. You'll also meet the amazing people who work there now, and a few game-changing people from our past.

THE STORY OF GCHQ:
Our amazing origins

But before I get to that, let's start at the very beginning. During the First World War, two codebreaking teams were set up to work out secret German messages. They were so successful at breaking the codes, that at the end of the war they formed one top secret organisation known as the Government Code & Cypher School (or GC&CS for short). They started work right away at their headquarters at Watergate House in London.

Today a plaque marks this location, which was unveiled with a little help from Her Majesty Queen Elizabeth in 2019. **Can you spot the secret messages in it?**

CITY OF WESTMINSTER
1919 - 1921
THE FIRST HOME OF
GCHQ
THE UK'S INTELLIGENCE, SECURITY AND CYBER AGENCY
KNOWN THEN AS GC&CS, FORMED FROM THE ADMIRALTY'S ROOM 40 AND THE WAR OFFICE'S MI1(b)
GCHQ CENTENARY 1919- 2019

At the start of the Second World War, they moved to Bletchley Park. This was a highly secretive site where amazing men and women (including most famously Alan Turing) worked around the clock to help break the secret Enigma and Lorenz codes being used by enemy forces to keep their messages secret. It is suggested that the painstaking work that went into breaking the codes shortened the war by many years.

In fact, it wasn't until much later that the world learnt about the incredible work that went on at Bletchley Park. You can visit there today – it's a fascinating day out!

11 A-maze-ing challenge

The maze below has several solutions.

Can you find the path with the shortest overall distance?

ENTRANCE

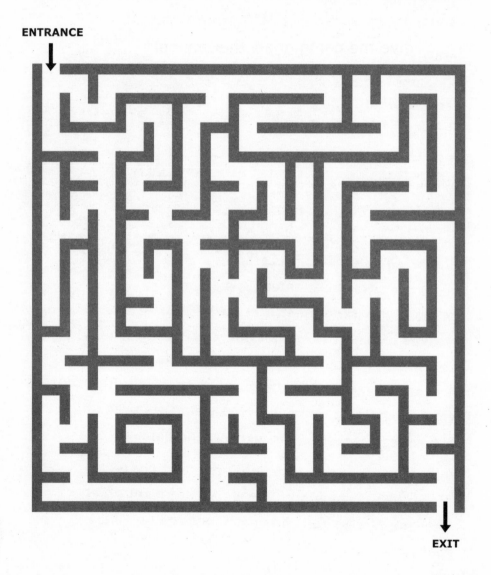

EXIT

12 Animal-agram

a) Which six of these words are anagrams of animals?

b) Which six can have one letter changed to give the name of another animal?

c) Which three words are in the answers to both part a) and part b)?

BARGED   **BOLSTER**   **BRAVER**

CAMEO   **HEAR**   **HEROS**

MUFFIN   **PAROLED**   **SWAP**

13 Odd one in

There can be lots of different reasons why a word might be the odd one out in a list. One reason might be because of the meaning of the word.

Which of these is the odd one out?

a) BANANA, CHERRY, HOUSE, LEMON, WATERMELON

Or maybe the reason is something about the word itself – such as a particular letter, or the number of letters – being different.

Which word is the odd one out in each list below?

b) PEACH, PEAR, PINEAPPLE, PLUM, STRAWBERRY

c) APPLE, GOOSEBERRY, GUAVA, MANGO, MELON

d) APRICOT, BLACKCURRANT, GRAPEFRUIT, REDCURRANT, TANGERINE

Let's finish with an odd one IN puzzle! Four of these words could be an odd one out – but which is *not* an odd one out?

e) GLOUCESTER, WARRINGTON, WINCHESTER, WOODPECKER, WORCESTER

PEOPLE FROM OUR PAST

NAME:

Alfred Dillwyn (Dilly) Knox

ROLE:

Codebreaker

FACT:

Dilly Knox was one of the first minds recruited to GC&CS. He even mentored codebreaking genius Alan Turing when he first arrived at Bletchley Park.

DID YOU KNOW?

He claimed he did his best thinking while sitting in the bathtub, so he used one in the middle of his office!

14 The right key

Find out which keys correspond to which notes
(letters), and use the numbers to put the letters
in order to reveal the words.

a)

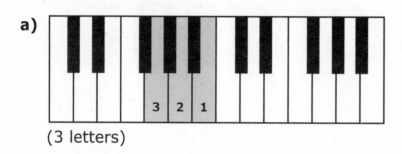

(3 letters)

b)

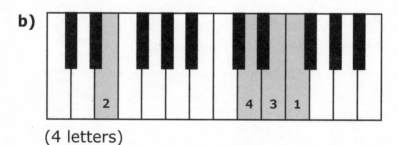

(4 letters)

c)

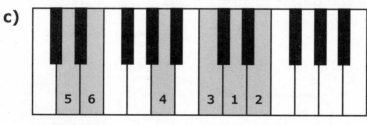

(6 letters)

For these final two we haven't given you the letter order so you'll have to find the letters and put them together yourselves to find the word!

d)

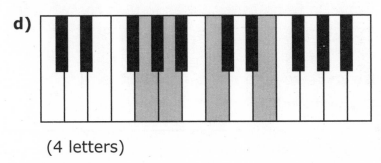

(4 letters)

And finally, identify this person, who was instrumental in the development of computers:

e)

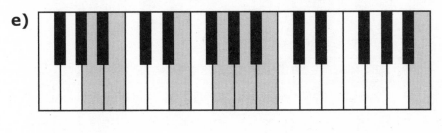

(7 letters)

You'll need to know which key is which on a piano. The hints on page 36 will help you.

15 The serpent

Solve the clues and put the answers into the grid.
When you put the answers in, you need to write
the Across answers from left to right, and the Down
answers from top to bottom, just as in the crossword in
Puzzle 7.

All the answers have different numbers of letters, so
there is only one place to put each answer.

- Huge biblical ship built by Noah to rescue
  animals from the flood. (3)
- Girl explorer with a talking backpack. (4)
- A word meaning twelve – or thirteen
  for bakers! (5)
- Long version of bye. (7)
- Informal name for the Loch Ness Monster. (6)
- Person from – or language of – Norway. (9)
- Spotting, observing, paying attention to. (8)
- Eastern Canadian province. (4, 6)
- Abbreviation for okay. (2)

When you have solved the grid, you will see a
word has appeared in the grey squares. What is it?

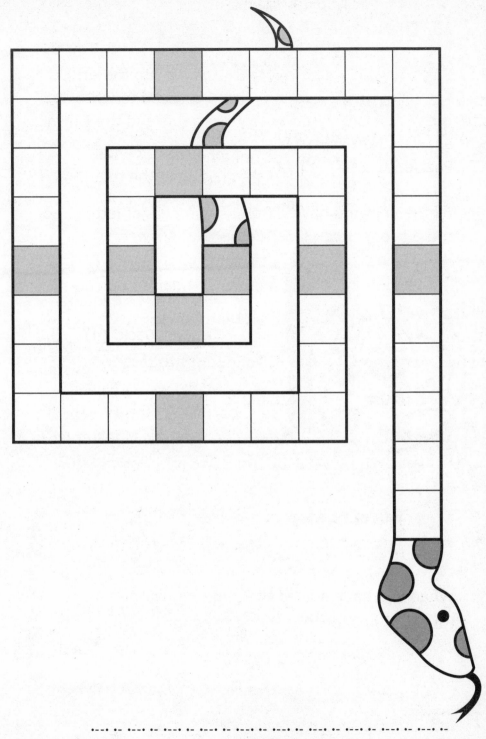

FUN FACTS

· ·

It wasn't until 1982 that the public knew we existed. Imagine that! A whole organisation doing incredible things, but we couldn't tell anyone about it.

Now, our huge headquarters is on the outskirts of Cheltenham. We affectionately call it The Doughnut because of its shape! It's a place we've called home for nearly twenty years.

At all of our locations across the UK, you'll find coffee shops, restaurants and even a well-known high street bakery. It's important to keep our hard-working staff well fed. You'll find we also have a top secret gym!

·--·- ·- ·--·- ·- ·--·- ·- ·--·- ·- ·--·- ·- ·--·- ·- ·--·- ·- ·--·- ·- ·--·- ·- ·--·- ·-

16 Bird brain

Did you know that a **ptarmigan** is a type of bird?

Can you find it and five other birds using the letters hiding in this brain, by going through the maze from Entrance to Exit via different routes?

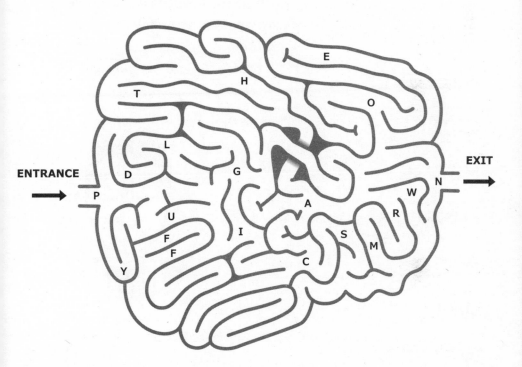

ENTRANCE →

EXIT →

There are many ways to complete the maze – see if you can get through it only travelling through the letters that spell out a particular bird. This is a tricky one, so check the hints on page 36 if you need to!

17 Maze message

Find these features hidden in the wordsearch maze opposite:

ARCHWAY

BOG

BEEHIVES

CLIFF

HEDGE

INSECTS

POND

WALL

WATERFALL

This is no ordinary wordsearch and some of the words may not go simply up and down or side to side. Check the hints on page 37 if you get stuck!

Can you find a path around these obstacles, starting from the middle of the ARCHWAY? (It will help if you colour the words you find!)

What message does it reveal?

E	H	F	U	O	Y	Y	A	Y
G	E	O	T	E	R	F	R	A
A	D	U	A	F	I	A	O	W
S	G	N	W	F	L	L	O	H
S	E	D	T	H	C	L	G	C
E	M	P	O	E	W	B	O	R
I	T	D	N	S	A	E	S	A
N	E	R	C	E	L	V	B	E
S	E	C	T	S	L	I	H	E

18 Spot-the-difference – animal edition

Can you find eight differences split between both of these pictures?

Once you've found the differences, use the letters around the edge of the grid to find the names of two birds that **aren't** in the pictures.

19 Tea and snake

1　　　　　**2**　　　　　**3**

Hassan, Tia and Wesley each live in one of these houses. Each one drinks either apple juice, hot chocolate or Earl Grey tea. And each one owns either a snake, an otter or an alligator.

Using the clues opposite, can you fill in the table to show who lives where, what they drink and what pet they own?

HOUSE NUMBER	NAME	DRINK	PET
1			
2			
3			

Can you find and answer the hidden question?

Clues

- Wesley doesn't own the alligator
- The apple juice drinker lives to the left of the Earl Grey tea drinker
- The hot chocolate drinker has an otter
- Tia lives to the right of Hassan
- The snake lives at an even number
- Hassan has two neighbours

You might want to use the table below to help you figure out who lives where. You can use ticks to show a relationship that you know, e.g. in the box for otter/hot chocolate, and crosses to show where you know there isn't a relationship, e.g. in the box for Wesley/alligator.

	1	2	3	Apple juice	Earl Grey tea	Hot chocolate	Alligator	Otter	Snake
Hassan									
Tia									
Wesley									
Aligator									
Otter									
Snake									
Apple juice									
Earl Grey tea									
Hot chocolate									

20 At sixes and sevens

The list of words in the left-hand column of the table opposite come from four groups of six words.

a) Can you identify the themes of the four groups?

Each word in this group then has a word that can be linked to it in the same way as the examples shown.

b) Can you work out all these linked words?

c) Can you then figure out where **LAMB** goes in the left-hand list?

At GCHQ, we call these **Where?** puzzles, and they are a style of puzzle that is unique to us.

WORD	LINKED WORD
FORWARD	BACKWARD
BRUSSELS	
KITTEN	
CALF	
PUPPY	DOG
UP	
OCTAGON	EIGHT
PENTAGON	
SQUARE	
PARIS	FRANCE
BERLIN	
KID	
FOAL	
ROME	
IN	
LISBON	
LEFT	
HEPTAGON	
HEXAGON	
MADRID	
TRIANGLE	
BOTTOM	
OVER	

Hints

1   To find the first animal, you have to change the T to a P, to get LEOPARD.

2   Start by looking at the number of letters in each month . . .

3   Some of these words can look difficult at first! But try going through them letter by letter, to see if you can uncover the hidden word.

4   The answer has been started for you.

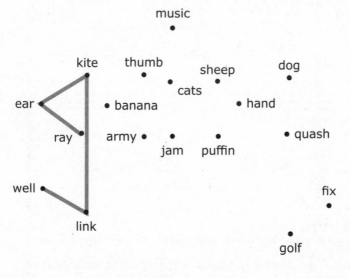

5   The last line of the limerick tells you how to solve the puzzle!

6 The odd row/column out does contain a body part –
but it's not one you'll find on a human!

7 The answer to 5 across is PANAMA. Can you see a
pattern in that word? Maybe the other answers are
similar?

8 The answer has been started below.

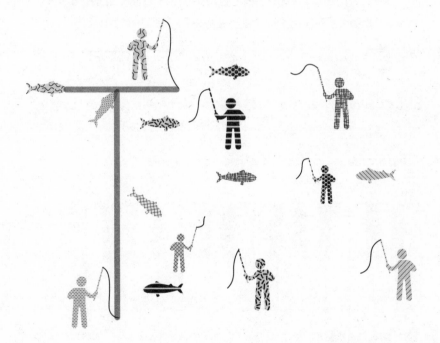

9 To work out the words in each list, try doing the
following. For part **a)**, add a letter to the beginning
of each word. For part **b)**, a letter needs to be added
in two places.

10 THY TWEETING has the same letters as TWENTY EIGHT. Maybe the other words can also be made into numbers?

11 To get the shortest route you don't want to go back on yourself at all. So can you find a route where you always go either right or down, but never left or up?

12 As an example, HEAR is an anagram of HARE. You can also change the first letter to get BEAR. This means HEAR is an answer to part **a)** and part **b)**, and so is one of the three words in part **c)**.

13 For part **a)**, can you find a word that is not a fruit? For parts **b)** and **c)** does one of the words just look out of place? For part **d)** consider the various types of differences already used

14 This picture shows which letter corresponds to which key.

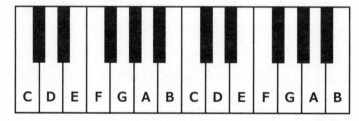

15 The answer to the clue 'Long version of bye' is GOODBYE. This should be written in the lowest horizontal bar, from left to right, which has 7 spaces. You'll see that the letter in the grey space is a D.

16 One of the other birds is PELICAN. In fact, all of the birds begin with the letter P and end with the letter N.

17 You can find the ARCHWAY in the last column. The path begins at the H, which can be found in the middle of the ARCHWAY. You can also find BEEHIVES, starting just below the A of ARCHWAY.

18 See the rhino in the bottom left of the picture? If you look carefully, you'll notice it has a little horn in the first picture but not in the second one. This difference is in the square which is in row F and column L. Write these down as FL, and then see what other pairs of letters you can find in the same way.

19 Using the final clue, you should be able to tell where Hassan lives.

20 The examples show how each group is linked to the other words. The cities are linked to the countries of which they are capitals. The directions are linked to their opposites. The baby animals are linked to their parent animal. The shapes are linked to their number of sides. And when the linked words are written out, they are in a certain order, which should tell you where LAMB goes . . .

You'll find the answers at the back of the book!

Chapter Two

LANGUAGES

A trip around the world

Hey puzzlers! My name is Rose and I'm a technical linguist at GCHQ's Cheltenham headquarters. That means I use my knowledge of languages other than English to help with our mission. I speak three different languages and am currently learning a fourth in my spare time.

Languages are hugely important to the people who work at GCHQ. They provide us with amazing opportunities and insights into many different countries. Knowing different languages also helps us to protect the UK from threats around the world, as GCHQ receives a lot of information and some of it isn't in English. This means it needs translating and generally making sense of so we can understand it properly.

When I was in my final two years of school, I didn't know what I wanted to study, or do for work. Then I discovered apprenticeships, including ones at GCHQ. An apprenticeship would mean I'd be able to work at GCHQ, and get a degree at the same time – so I would be paid while I was studying.

Then I found out that GCHQ is one of the UK's intelligence agencies. *I could be a spy, I thought to myself,* which sounded pretty cool!

Because I had learnt the skills to be a technical apprentice, I became a technical linguist. That means combining my technical ability, language skills and knowledge of different countries. The best way I can describe it is like this: imagine explaining how to build a website . . . now imagine explaining how to build a website, but in Arabic. That's basically what my job is like!

Translations can be challenging. Sometimes words in other languages have lots of different meanings that change depending on the situation they're used in. Maybe you've noticed that when you're learning languages at school? Language analysts must have a deep understanding of different countries – the ideas, the behaviour, the culture and even the slang – as only then can we really understand what's being said.

Sometimes people even try to hide what they are talking about by using words we might not recognize. It can be frustrating trying to work these out if you have never seen a word or phrase used in that way before. But it is rewarding once you crack it! So really, learning a language is a bit like breaking a code. A really complex – but completely amazing – code.

I have a neurodiversity called ADHD, which means I sometimes find it hard to stay focused. It also means I can process information quickly. This helps me a lot in my job. I regularly get to use the skills I am good at, such as problem solving and pattern spotting.

You'll be doing lots of this in your next puzzling adventure. We're heading off round the world, looking at lots of different languages. Some of them are similar to English, and some have even borrowed words from English, just like we have borrowed words from languages such as French and Latin. Some languages use alphabets that English doesn't have, which might make the puzzles very tricky, but very interesting.

Bonne chance, puzzlers.
(*Bonne chance* means good luck in French!)

Rose

Before you set off on your travels, you need a passport – and every good spy needs a secret identity.

Fill in your brand-new pretend passport below. You can even have a go at drawing yourself (plus a disguise, of course) where your passport photo will go!

PASSPORT

NAME ....

DREAM JOB ....

FAVOURITE HOLIDAY DESTINATION

....

NUMBER OF LANGUAGES SPOKEN

....

2524443927642/663

As you voyage through these language puzzles, you'll want to keep track of where you've been. Tick the box next to the stamp in your passport when you've completed the puzzle for that country.

CHILE ☐

FRANCE ☐

EGYPT ☐

THE NETHERLANDS ☐

ARGENTINA ☐

SOUTH AFRICA ☐

GERMANY ☐

NIGERIA ☐

UNITED KINGDOM ☐

JAPAN ☐

GREECE ☐

1 Cracking packing

We're going to start our journey in the United Kingdom.
Every traveller needs a suitcase to pack their things in –
but yours has been locked!

Each lock starts and ends with a word, and you need to
get from the top to the bottom of each lock by changing
one letter to make a different word each time.

Can you work out the missing words to crack each
of the three locks and open the suitcase?

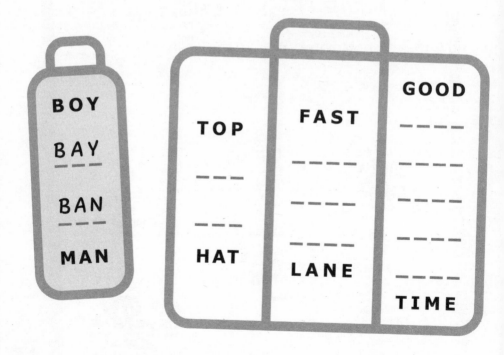

BOY

BAY
– – –

BAN
– – –

MAN

TOP

– – –

– – –

HAT

FAST

– – – –

– – – –

– – – –

LANE

GOOD

– – – –

– – – –

– – – –

– – – –

– – – –

TIME

2 First stop

Our first stop is France. When you start learning languages, it is useful to spot patterns.

Here are some sentences in French:

Le lapin est dans le jardin. *Le lapin est dans la maison.*
The rabbit is in the garden. The rabbit is in the house.

Le chat est dans le jardin. *Le chien est dans la maison.*
The cat is in the garden. The dog is in the house.

Using the sentences and words above, can you now make your own sentences in French?

a) The cat is in the house.
Le .... *est dans la* ....

b) The dog is in the garden.
Le .... *est*
dans le ....

Try speaking these out loud!

3 From Paris to Berlin

Guten Tag, junger Rätsellöser!
This means **Hello, young puzzle solver** in German!

Next we're heading to Germany.
In German, sometimes there are long words
which are made up of several individual words.

These can look really complicated to begin with,
but if you start by breaking down the long word into
smaller words, it can help you understand it.

For example:

Kinder means 'children', and **Buch** means 'book',
so **Kinderbuch** means 'children's book'.

Here's another one:

Wasser means 'water', and **Kocher** means 'cooker',
so **Wasserkocher** means 'kettle' (because a kettle
'cooks' water).

Can you work out the following words, using the translations for the individual words?

   a) **Hand** means 'hand', and **Schuh** means 'shoe', so what does **Handschuh** mean?

   b) **Regen** means 'rain', and **Schirm** means 'shield', so what does **Regenschirm** mean?

   c) **Tier** means 'animal', and **Arzt** means 'doctor', so what does **Tierarzt** mean?

   d) **Flug** means 'fly' or 'flight', and **Zeug** means 'thing', so what does **Flugzeug** mean?

••• •• •• ••••• ••• ••• •• ••• •• •• •••• ••• ••• •• ••

4 Going Dutch

A hop, skip and a jump from Germany is the Netherlands. It's very close in distance to Germany, and the languages also have some similarities.

We are going to learn to count to ten in Dutch.

1	een
2	twee
3	drie
4	vier
5	vijf
6	zes
7	zeven
8	acht
9	negen
10	tien

Using the numbers on the left can you translate the following?

a) Drie boeken
b) Zeven kinderen
c) Acht schoenen
d) Twee dieren

You might think the Dutch words are tricky to work out. But as Dutch is actually very similar to German, the previous question might help you. If it's still too hard, try the hints on page 73.

PEOPLE FROM OUR PAST

NAME:

Brigadier John Tiltman

ROLE:

Codebreaker

FACT:

Awarded the Military Cross for his service during the First World War, John had impressive codebreaking skills. He went on to set up the military section at Bletchley Park, the source of many key breakthroughs during the Second World War.

DID YOU KNOW?

In the military, John quickly realised the importance of partnerships. After the war he helped to set up an intelligence sharing relationship with the USA, which still exists today, over seventy-five years later. It helps keep both countries safe by allowing them to share secret information with each other.

5 Ancient lingo

Hope you've packed your sunscreen, because you have now arrived in Athens, the capital city of Greece. The first thing you'll notice is that the Greek alphabet is very different to the English one. Don't panic though, as you might recognize some letters.

- Π is the pi symbol in maths, and also the letter P.
- Σ is the letter S (you can see that they look quite similar).
- Some Greek letters look like English alphabet letters but are actually different. For example, the Greek letter P is the English R and the Greek letter Y is close to U in English.
- Some Greek letters represent two letters in the English alphabet.

You might have heard myths and stories about the Greek gods and goddesses – well, here are some of their names written in the Greek alphabet. Using the tips above, can you match them to the gods and goddesses on the opposite page?

ΑΦΡΟΔΙΤΗ	ΖΕΥΣ	ΠΟΣΕΙΔΩΝΑΣ
ΓΗ	ΚΡΟΝΟΣ	ΣΕΛΗΝΗ
ΑΡΗΣ	ΟΥΡΑΝΟΣ	ΠΛΟΥΤΩΝΑΣ

GE (Gaia)
Earth Goddess

ARES (Ares)
God of war

POSEIDONAS
(Poseidon)
God of the sea

OURANOS (Uranus)
God of the night sky

KRONOS (Cronus)
God of time

PLOUTONAS
(Pluto) God of
the underworld

ZEUS (Zeus)
God of the sky

SELENE (Selene)
Goddess of the moon

APHRODITE
(Aphrodite)
God of love

6 Chatting in Arabic

Now we are off to Egypt! Here we are going to learn how to speak some **Arabic**.

The formal way to say hello in Arabic is:

As-Salaam Alaykum

This actually means **peace be upon you**, and is not only used in countries which speak Arabic, but also by Muslims all over the world.

To reply, you say:

Wa Alaykum as-Salaam

This means **and upon you be peace**.

> **a)** The Arabic for **my name is** sounds a bit like **it's me** in English. Can you work out which of these phrases is the Arabic for **my name is**?
>
> **Kalbi**   **Ismi**   **Qitati**

b) Can you now work out which of these phrases means **her name is**?

Ismha   **Sadiquha**   **Baytuha**

c) Now read the following conversation:

Ali: As-Salaam Alaykum Fatima!
Fatima: Wa Alaykum as-Salaam Ali!
Ali: Kayf al-Hal?
Fatima (smiling): Mumtaz. Kayf al-Hal?
Ali (frowning): Hazin

From this conversation, can you work out the Arabic for **how are you**?

Can you also find the Arabic words for **sad** and **excellent**?

Now you too can have a conversation with a friend in Arabic!

Arabic is commonly written using different characters. For example, As-Salaam Alaykum is written as السلام عليكم

7 Flying to Japan

The Japanese language actually has several alphabets, but we are going to look at one of them called **hiragana**, which is used to spell words as they sound.

Here are some words in **hiragana**. You can see how each symbol in the word corresponds to a sound, and when they are put together they tell you how to say the word. We've put the translation next to each word.

えだまめ
e da ma me = *Soya beans*

きもの
ki mo no = *National dress*

おりがみ
o ri ga mi = *Art of paper folding*

さつま
sa tsu ma = *Small citrus fruit*

ふとん
fu to n = *Traditional Japanese bed*

いけばな
i ke ba na = *Art of flower arranging*

さけ
sa ke = *Rice wine for drinking*

すし
su shi = *Cold rice dish*

ひじき
hi ji ki = *Edible seaweed*

みりん
mi ri n = *Rice wine for cooking*

さむらい
sa mu ra i = *Samurai warrior*

すうどく
su u do ku = *Sudoku puzzle*

••▪- -▪• •• ▪••▪ --- -▪• -- ▪▪- -▪ •• ▪▪•▪ --- -▪• -- ▪▪- -▪ •• ▪••▪ --- -▪• --

Below is a wordsearch in **hiragana**.

a) Find all the words listed opposite.

い	ら	む	さ	し	え	ふ
く	ど	う	す	つ	だ	と
ひ	さ	え	も	じ	ま	ん
じ	い	け	ば	な	め	り
き	も	の	お	り	が	み

Don't forget to look forwards, backwards, up, down and diagonally!

b) Which symbols are left over, and what sounds do they make? What modern language does this spell?

THE STORY OF GCHQ:
Learning the lingo

GCHQ works with countries around the world, so being able to speak different languages is really important in our mission to keep our country safe.

As an organisation with a global mission, linguists provide translations, data and vital insight wherever in the world it is needed.

During the Second World War, as well as breaking German codes, we also had to break Japanese ones. But we soon realised that there was a shortage of people in the UK who spoke Japanese!

Early GCHQ workers needed to change this, and eventually the brilliant John Tiltman came up with a plan to make sure enough people in the organisation could learn Japanese to help break the codes.

Nowadays, linguists across the organisation are

able to speak over **sixty** different languages and dialects between them. Of course, many people at GCHQ speak languages that they don't necessarily use in their job! Often linguists learn cultural differences – and even slang – to give them the context they need to accurately translate material.

Just think how different parts of the UK refer to a bread roll: a barm, butty, bap, cob. We find languages truly fascinating!

Hello!
hola
bonjour
guten tag
salve
nǐn hǎo
olá
As-Salaam Alaykum
konnichiwa
anyoung haseyo

8 It's time for Africa

Next stop: Africa! This huge continent is home to many countries and languages.

Hausa is a language spoken in West Africa, especially in northern Nigeria. The alphabet is mostly like English, but there are a few letters with 'hooks' on them. One of these is a hooked d, which looks like this: ɗ. You say it like a normal d, but stronger, and with the tip of your tongue touching the ridge behind your top front teeth.

Try saying the words opposite with the ɗ correctly pronounced – it's always important to practise saying the new words you learn!

Here are numbers 1–15 in **Hausa**.

1 – ɗaya

2 – biyu

3 – uku

4 – huɗu

5 – biyar

6 – shida

7 – bakwai

8 – takwas

the 'wai' part
rhymes with 'eye'

9 – tara

10 – goma

11 – (goma) sha ɗaya

12 – (goma) sha biyu

13 – (goma) sha uku

14 – (goma) sha huɗu

15 – (goma) sha biyar

you can say these
numbers with the word
'goma' or without it

Now here are some simple sums. Can you give the answers in **Hausa**?

a) 2 + 6 = ...

b) 9 – 4 = ...

c) takwas + uku = ...

d) uku × uku = ...

e) sha biyu ÷ biyu = ...

f) takwas × biyu = ...

g) shida × uku = ...

You won't see the answers to the last two in
the list above. But using the numbers we've given
you, do you think you can work them out?

In **Hausa**, numbers from twenty upwards are formed like this:

20 – ishirin

21 – ishirin da ɗaya

22 – ishirin da biyu

23 – ishirin da uku

24 – ishirin da huɗu

25 – ishirin da biyar

this can also be said or written as 'ashirin'

the word 'da' in these numbers means 'and', so the number 21 is like saying 'twenty and one'

Here are the other multiples of ten in **Hausa**:

30 – talatin

40 – arba'in

50 – hamsin

60 – sittin

70 – saba'in

80 – tamanin

90 – casa'in

you say words ending with **'in** in two parts: 'arba-in'

c in Hausa is like 'ch' in English, so this sounds like 'chasa-in'

Using these numbers and the ones you have seen before, can you give the answers to the sums below in **Hausa**?

h) 15 + 7 = ...

i) 10 × 4 = ...

j) talatin – uku = ...

k) sittin da takwas ÷ biyu = ...

l) talatin da uku + sittin da shida = ...

m) bakwai × takwas = ...

Now you should know all the numbers in Hausa from 1–99. As a bonus, here is number 100 – ɗari

9 Yes you Afrikaan!

This means 'fantastic' in Afrikaans!

Our final stop in Africa is *lekker*. It's South Africa! Here, lots of people speak Afrikaans – a language similar to Dutch.

Upon your arrival in Cape Town, you are given a map in Afrikaans and need to plot your way round the city. First, you need to work out what some Afrikaans words and directions mean in English.

What do you think the following Afrikaans directions mean in English?

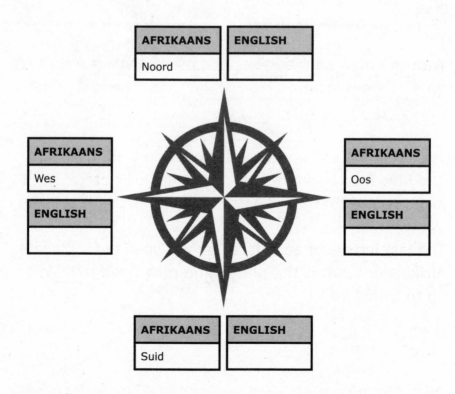

AFRIKAANS	ENGLISH
Noord	

AFRIKAANS
Wes

ENGLISH

AFRIKAANS
Oos

ENGLISH

AFRIKAANS	ENGLISH
Suid	

Go back to page 48
if you need a reminder!

Using the numbers you learned in Puzzle 4, can you work out what each of these Afrikaans numbers mean in English?

AFRIKAANS	ENGLISH
Vyf	
Ses	
Agt	
Drie	
Een	

AFRIKAANS	ENGLISH
Tien	
Twee	
Vier	
Nege	
Sewe	

With the map on the next page as your guide, navigate the city from location to location using the table under the map.

The table will tell you which way to go from the start, and how many squares to travel. Make a note of each place you visit and write its last letter in the table too.

The last letters of each location will spell out a place in Afrikaans. What is the place? You may need to look it up to translate it!

MAP

START			Park			Hotel
	Gym					
					Forest	
	Bus stop				Butcher's	
			Bank			
Museum						Zoo
	Cinema	Pond	Sauna		Spa	

TABLE

DIRECTION	ENGLISH	NUMBER OF SQUARES	ENGLISH	PLACE	LAST LETTER
oos		drie			
suid		nege			
wes		twee			
noord		vyf			
oos		vier			
noord		een			
suid		ses			
wes		drie			

10 Numero diez

The last location on our journey around the world is South America. This is a continent where Spanish is spoken in lots of countries, including Argentina.

Spanish, like French, has genders for nouns, which means words like table or shirt are either masculine or feminine.

Can you spot the gender patterns in the following table and use them to complete the blanks?

the house	la casa	my sister	mi hermana
the houses	las casas	your sister	tu hermana
my house	mi casa	our sisters	
your house	tu casa	our brother	nuestro hermano
our house	nuestra casa	my sisters	mis hermanas
the bicycle	la bicicleta	our English grandmother	nuestra abuela inglesa
your bicycles	tus bicicletas	your grandfathers	tus abuelos
my bicycle		our English house	nuestra casa inglesa
our tickets	nuestras entradas	your brothers	
the tickets		your English bicycle	
my job	mi trabajo	our jobs	
		your grandmothers	

11 Chill in Chile!

Using your navigational skills developed in the previous Afrikaans puzzle and your Spanish skills, solve the following puzzle:

MAP OF SANTIAGO

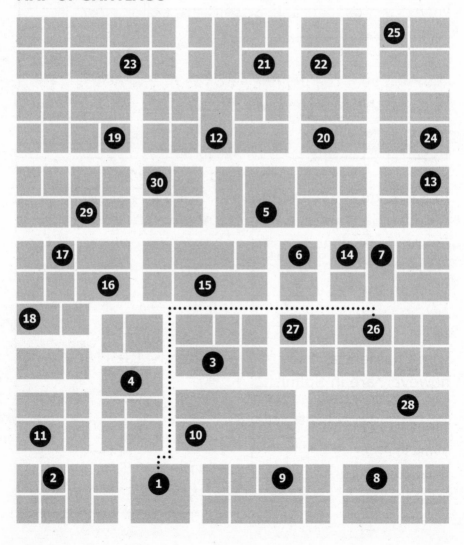

..._ _._ .. ..._ --- _._ _ ..._ _._ .. ..._ --- _._ _ ..._ _._ .. ..._ --- _._ _

KEY

1 Hotel María	**11** La Latina	**21** Barracudas
2 Café Roja	**12** Mercado	**22** La Chocita del Loro
3 Jardín de Especias	**13** Casa Museo Max Moreau	**23** Liberia Praga
4 Cafetería Indalo	**14** Zapatos Azules	**24** Clínica Radiológica
5 Hotel Elena	**15** Museo Sorolla	**25** Mundidulce
6 El Coso	**16** Teatro Real	**26** La Alborea
7 Patio de los Perfumes	**17** Kebab Ali Baba	**27** La Urbanita
8 Casa del Arte Flamenco	**18** Museo de Arte	**28** Bar Los Carmenes
9 Los Patos	**19** Tienda Souvenirs	**29** Tienda Souvenirs
10 Antojitos Comida de Mexicana	**20** Jardín de Zoraya	**30** Gelato Italiano

In Santiago, the capital city of Chile, you are staying in Hotel Maria (number 1 on the map). You are with some Spanish-speaking friends, and they have written a list of places to visit today along with the directions from one place to the next.

The first place you are going is **La Alborea**, to watch some flamenco dancing. The directions to get there, however, are in Spanish.

Gira a la derecha por la calle.

Toma la primera a la izquierda.

Toma la segunda a la derecha y sigue por la calle.

Pase el giro a la derecha y es el tercer edificio a la derecha.

You read them as you walk with your friends to La Alborea, and make note of the directions you travel:

Turn right down the street.
Take the first left.
Take the second right and continue down the street.
Pass the turn on the right and it is the third building on the right.

What are the Spanish words for:

ENGLISH	SPANISH
Right	
Left	
Building	
Street	
Take	

ENGLISH	SPANISH
First	
Second	
Third	
Turn	
Pass	

These words might have more than one ending in Spanish!

Unfortunately, after the show you lose your friends who have headed off to the next location. You only have the directions that begin at La Alborea.

Gira a la izquierda por la calle y toma la primera a la derecha.

Gira a la derecha y toma la primera a la izquierda.

Toma la primera a la derecha y es el segundo edifico a la derecha.

Using the directions on the previous page, work out where your friends went.

You still haven't found your friends, but you have a list of directions for where they went next.

> Gira a la izquierda por la calle.
>
> Toma la segunda a la derecha.
>
> Toma la primera a la izquierda.
>
> Es el primer edificio a la derecha.

What is the next destination your friends went to?

You still haven't found your friends! By the time you got to the next place, they'd moved on to the final destination for the evening. But you have some more directions . . .

> Gira a la derecha por la calle.
>
> Toma la primera a la izquierda.
>
> Toma la tercera a la derecha.
>
> Es el primer edifico a la derecha.

Where did your friends end up?

12 Finishing in style

There's just one more fiendish puzzle to go!

You've learned so much about languages by travelling round the world, but all of them have relied on sight or sound.

Braille is a written language that uses touch to read a series of dots. The dots are put into patterns that correspond to letters. They are always raised slightly so visually impaired people can read them.

For example this pattern ⠝ is the Braille character for **N**.

Opposite is a list of European cities written in Braille. Some of the cities are Rome, Vienna, Minsk and Copenhagen. Fill in their names.

⠝ ⠝

FUN FACTS

In the middle of the Doughnut we have a large courtyard. It's one of only a few outdoor gardens in the country where conversations are classified as top secret. It's so big, you could fit the whole of the Royal Albert Hall inside it.

Then there's the Data Centre, which is built deep underground. It's the nerve centre of GCHQ and houses a lot of the technical equipment that enables our work. It has enough cabling to stretch to the Moon and back, and many supercomputers.
It's the size of thirty-eight tennis courts!

Grab your trainers, because it would take sixty-five laps of the Doughnut to run the equivalent of a full marathon!

Hints

1 CAST your eyes over the second question to find the first word. For the third question, you'll be good as GOLD if you do what you're TOLD.

2 The words in the French sentences are in the same order as the words in the English sentences – and all the words you need are in the examples shown.

3 Try to imagine what a combination of the words might look like. For example, what sort of 'shoe' would you put on your hand?

4 These Dutch nouns have 'en' added to show they are plural, so it might be helpful to try looking at them without the 'en'. You might also be able to find similarities with both German and English words. For example, 'book' is 'Buch' in German, and 'boek' in Dutch.

5 Try to read the Greek names letter by letter. Where you don't know a letter, skip over it and see if you can then work out what it is from what you have left. For example, you know some of the letters in ΠΛΟΥΤΩΝΑΣ are P?OUT?NAS, so which name could that be? When you've found it, you can deduce which English letters are represented by Λ and Ω.

6 For parts **a)** and **b)** try saying each word out loud. For part **c)** try to imagine how a conversation might go in English.

7 You can find the sounds for the remaining symbols in the words already provided. Try putting the sounds together, and read them out loud to help you find the modern language!

8 Part **g)** translates to 6 × 3 = 18. To work out what 18 is in Hausa, look to see how 12, (goma) sha biyu, has been formed from the number 2, biyu, and then see if you can work out how 18 could be formed from 8, takwas.

9 In order, the numbers are: een, twee, drie, vier, vyf, ses, sewe, agt, nege, tien.

10 You can see that 'house' in Spanish is 'casa', and 'my house' is 'mi casa'. 'Bicycle' in Spanish is 'bicicleta', so 'my bicycle' is 'mi bicicleta'. Similarly, 'the houses' is 'las casas', and 'tickets' is 'entradas', so 'the tickets' is 'las entradas'.

11 For the first part of this question, you know that 'Gira a la derecha por la calle' means 'Turn right down the street', as indicated by the directions on the map and the English directions you've been given. 'Toma la primera a la izquierda', therefore, by comparison, means 'Take the first left'. Continue to follow the line, and look at the English instructions, and compare them with the Spanish instructions to work out what 'segunda' means, and see how 'third building' has been translated.

12 The tenth line is ⠠⠉⠕⠏⠑⠝⠓⠁⠛⠑⠝, which is the only line with 10 characters – and so must translate to Copenhagen. You can see the letter ⠝ (which is N) is in it twice too, as you'd expect. So you can deduce that in Braille C= ⠉, O= ⠕, P= ⠏, E= ⠑, H= ⠓, A= ⠁ and G= ⠛. Now you can use these letters to work out the other cities.

Chapter Three

ENGINEERING

Building your robot

Hello, puzzlers! My name is Shanti. There are lots of different types of engineers at GCHQ, including mechanical, electrical and software. I'm a software engineer.

Software is a program on a computer that makes it work. In my team our work normally involves coding. I write instructions using languages that computers understand, to tell them what action to take – this is the code. The whole process is called engineering (or creating) new software. There's more on coding in the Coding chapter on page 198.

We code software so our computers can do certain things. Then we share what we've created with teams across GCHQ to support the important work they do to keep the country safe. Our software has been essential to the success of many different operations that have been carried out – though sadly I can't tell you about a lot of them as they're TOP SECRET!

So how did I get here? I was looking for jobs after graduating with a degree in computer science, when my friend told me about GCHQ. I always wanted to do something that would make a difference. So I crossed my fingers and applied. After being interviewed, thankfully I was offered the job.

At school, maths was my favourite subject. At the other end of the scale, art was my favourite hobby! Very different, right? I loved doing anything creative – particularly drawing and painting – and I spent my free time either hanging out with my friends or listening to music, while drawing anything and everything.

Software engineering has really let me have the best of both worlds. I love the maths and other challenges involved with writing software, but I also love the creative side – developing new software requires me to think outside the box.

In my current role, I work from GCHQ's Cheltenham headquarters. However, I regularly visit our London office, and I like travelling to meet my engineering colleagues in Scarborough, North Yorkshire, too. Although we're based in different locations, it's important we work together and learn from each other.

The hardest thing about my role is that there is never a 'one size fits all' solution. Every problem, and every piece of software, requires you to think differently, and while that can be challenging at times, it's still the best part of the job. You never get bored.

Engineering involves designing and building things. Not just software, but everything from computer chips to robots! In this chapter, we're going to build a robot together, with help from my colleagues who are mechanical and electrical engineers.

Each puzzle in this chapter will help us on our way to building the most amazing robot step by step! The robot design might change from question to question, but don't worry. As engineers, we often change designs completely when we're working on a project, in case something doesn't work.

For this chapter, I suggest you get a pen, paper and some scissors, as a lot of the puzzles require you to fit things together, or move shapes around to find the solution. For instance, step 12 involves moving blocks from different boxes, and I think you'll find it a lot easier if you draw each shape and cut them out, and try moving them by hand. In engineering, we often have to solve problems by trying our ideas out on paper first. You can give designing your own a go on page 108.

Shanti

STEP 1 Fresh out of the box

The first thing I need to do is unlock my box of robot designs. To open the box, I need to combine the shapes below (numbered 1 to 8) to make images **A**, **B** and **C**. The shapes need to combine exactly to form the images, and they can't overlap.

Can you help me work out which shapes combine to form each image?

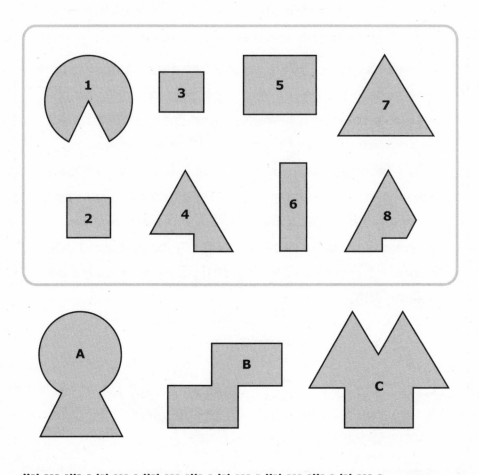

STEP 2 Grand designs

In the box are three designs, but only one has all the requirements I need for my mission! Can you help me find which one to use?

Requirements:

- It needs more wheels than arms.
- Speed is more important than strength.
- Night vision would be nice, but not essential.
- Battery life needs to be at least as good as strength.

ROBOT 1

Speed:	★★★☆☆
Strength:	★★★★☆
Battery Life:	★★★★☆
Night Vision:	**NO**

ROBOT 2

Speed:	★★★★☆
Strength:	★★★☆☆
Battery Life:	★★★☆☆
Night Vision:	**NO**

ROBOT 3

Speed:	★★★★★
Strength:	★★★★☆
Battery Life:	★★★☆☆
Night Vision::	**YES**

STEP 3 Side by side

We've got an idea for a robot design, but in order to make it properly, we need to know what it looks like from the side. This is the robot from the front.

Which image below shows what it would look like from the side?

A

B

C

D

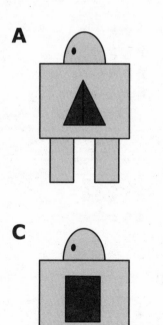

STEP 4 Prototype

I've come up with another idea for how the robot could look. How many of each of the shapes below do we need to build the robot design?

A  **B** **C** **D**

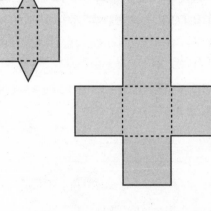

SHAPE	QUANTITY
A	
B	
C	
D	

When solving this, imagine folding the shape templates along the dashed lines to make 3D shapes.

STEP 5 Ronnie, Romy and Rowan

I was so excited when I received designs for some robot faces – named Ronnie, Romy and Rowan – that I totally forgot to label them!

All I can remember is that Ronnie's face has more different types of shape than Romy's, but Romy has more pieces in total than Ronnie.

Can you name the robots using this information?

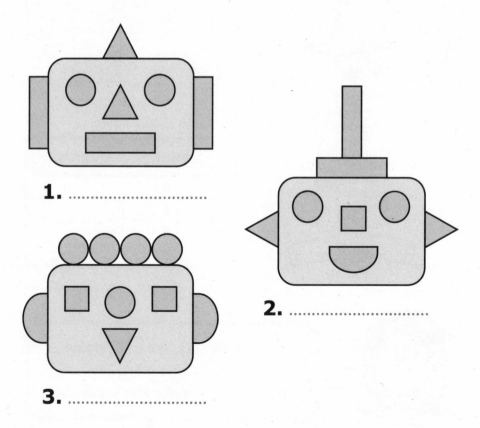

1. ....

2. ....

3. ....

STEP 6 Missing parts

I'd gathered all the parts to make models of my robot faces, but then dropped them all over the floor! I think I might have lost some of the smaller pieces, though I still have the three big blocks with the rounded corners.

This is what's left. It looks like there are still plenty to make at least one of Ronnie, Romy and Rowan's faces, but are there enough to complete two – and if so, whose?

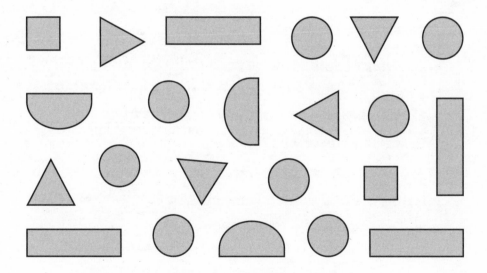

THE STORY OF GCHQ:
Great gadgets

GCHQ's top secret work needs awesome, top secret gadgets . . . and we've had some pretty amazing ones over the years.

Our engineers at GCHQ often need to make sure the messages of some very important people can't be read or listened to – even the Royal Family! A lot of this has involved making sure telephone calls can't be intercepted (we call this making the calls **secure**).

In the 1950s, the Soviet Union had put dangerous missiles in Cuba, which were able to reach America, and it started a crisis that could have led to another world war. A bright red phone called the PICKWICK was developed, which allowed the British Prime Minister Harold Macmillan to speak to the United States President John F. Kennedy without anyone listening in, which helped them sort the crisis out!

Another special phone was developed in the 1980s for the British Prime Minister Margaret Thatcher. She needed a secure phone that could be easily carried around, and would fit in a small briefcase. This was so, when she was out and about, she could make a secure phone call, even when she was on holiday! A machine was invented that looked like a briefcase, but contained inside it a telephone that the Prime Minister could use for top secret conversations. This invention was called the BRAHMS telephone.

PICKWICK telephone

BRAHMS telephone

STEP 7 The cogs are turning

In order for it to work,
we need cogs inside
our robot. The cogs
will either turn:

CLOCKWISE   **ANTICLOCKWISE**

If a cog turns clockwise, then the cog next to it turns
anticlockwise. If a cog turns anticlockwise, the one
next to it turns clockwise.

Using this information, can you figure out which
way cogs A and B will turn?

STEP 8 Crossed wires

When testing the robot, I noticed some of the wires had been connected incorrectly! Using the rules below, can you fix these wires in five steps?

There are **eight** mistakes in total.

- All wires must be connected.
- Wires must connect the top row to the bottom row.
- The pattern on the wire must match the pattern on the socket.
- Wires must not be twisted round other wires (though wires can cross over).

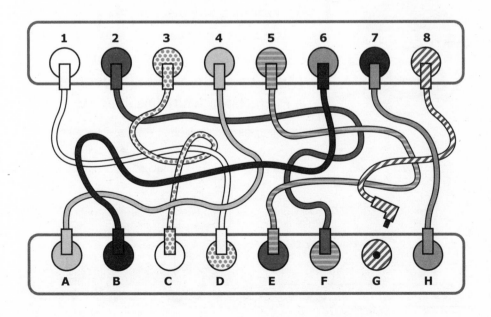

STEP 9 Circuit breaker

Our robot needs some circuit boards so it can run on electricity. Can you help me piece together the different components for the three boards?

A complete board is made up of four jigsaw pieces connected together, and our robot needs three separate complete circuit boards to work.

For two jigsaw pieces to fit together, all the white lines that show the circuits need to match up. The pieces cannot be rotated.

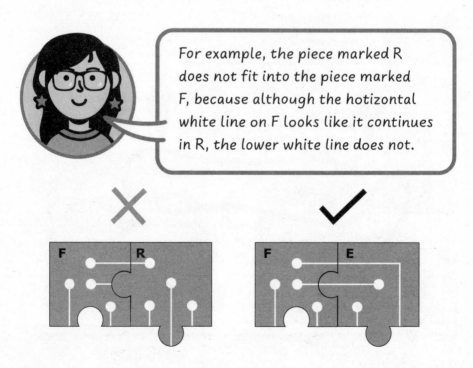

For example, the piece marked R does not fit into the piece marked F, because although the hotizontal white line on F looks like it continues in R, the lower white line does not.

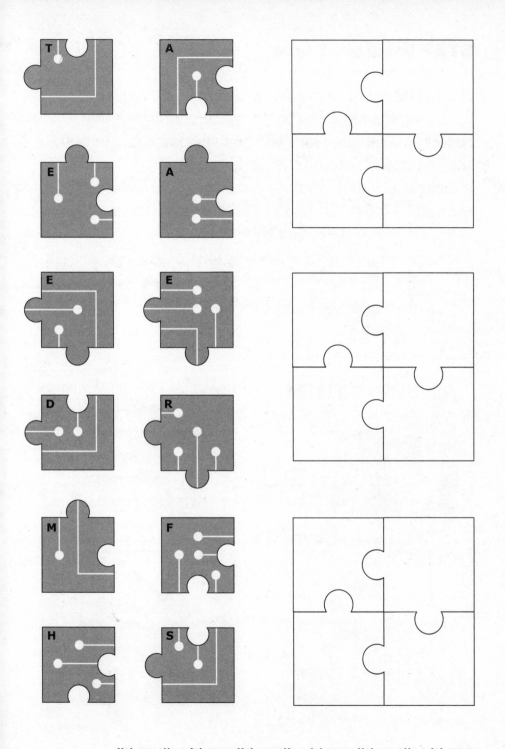

STEP 10 Robot race

It's now time to get to work and build our robot! This involves assembling the parts and wiring them together. Can you work out how quickly you can build the robot and wire all the parts together?

- There are three teams.
- Only one team can wire at a time.
- Only two teams can build at the same time – so one team could be building one part, while another team tackles another.

ASSEMBLY TIMES

Head = **10 DAYS**

Body = **6 DAYS**

Arms = **2 DAYS**

Wheels = **1 DAY**

WIRING TIMES

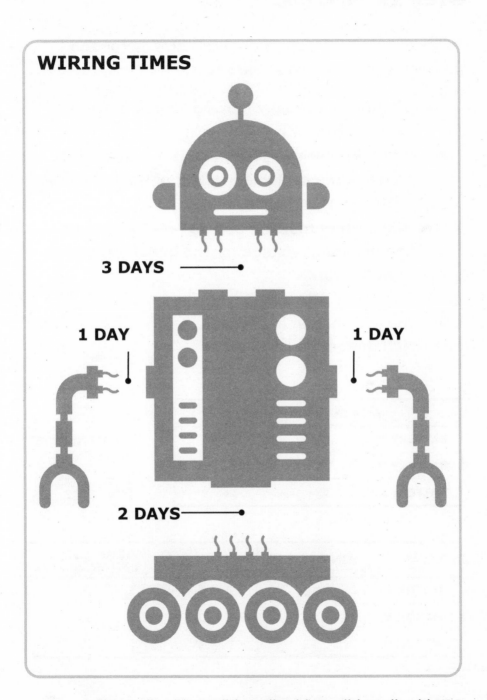

3 DAYS

1 DAY

1 DAY

2 DAYS

STEP 11 Power up

In order to move, our robot needs one motor and one battery. Here's what we know:

- The motor can only move a limited amount of weight.
- The robot weighs 10kg, and the motor needs to move the combined weight of the robot, the motor and the battery.
- The battery must be able to provide at least the minimum voltage for the motor, otherwise it won't work.

Using the information in the table below, which battery and which motor should I choose?

	VOLTAGE	WEIGHT (Kg)
BATTERY A	5	3
BATTERY B	12	5
BATTERY C	20	14

	MIN VOLTAGE	WEIGHT (Kg)	WEIGHT IT CAN MOVE (Kg)
MOTOR A	12	2	15
MOTOR B	20	10	30
MOTOR C	12	4	20

PEOPLE FROM OUR PAST

NAME:
Bill Tutte

ROLE:
Mathematician and codebreaker

FACT:

A fine mathematician in his own right, Bill was famous for teaming up with his friends to tackle almost impossible mathematical problems to help win the Second World War.

DID YOU KNOW?

Bill's most significant work was his discovery of how the Lorenz code machine worked. This was used by officers high up in the the German military to send secret messages. By cracking it, Bill ensured the United Kingdom and its allies could understand the messages being sent by their enemies.

STEP 12 Repair shop

Oh no! Our robot has sustained some damage and needs to be repaired. This will require moving four components **(A, B, C, D)** from slot 1 to slot 2.

There are certain rules you need to follow, though. You can only move the top component in a pile from one slot to another. And because of each component's weight, they can only be placed on top of a component that is larger (so **A** can be placed on any of **B**, **C** or **D**, but **D** always has to be the bottom component of the pile that it's in).

When completed, you need to end up with the components in slot 2 looking just like the ones in slot 1 now. Grab some different size coins to help you trial solutions.

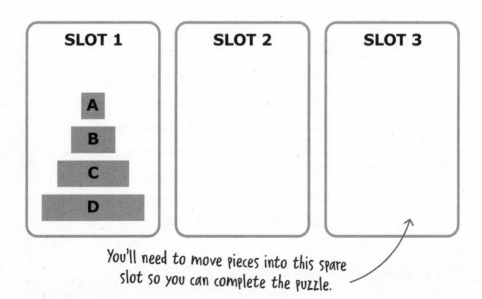

You'll need to move pieces into this spare slot so you can complete the puzzle.

STEP 13 On the move

The robot is now learning how to move, but can only remember four moves in one go. Possible moves are:

U: Up	**D: Down**	**R: Right**	**L: Left**

Help me put the moves below together so the robot can exit the maze without walking on the same square more than once.

RRUR _G   DRUR _I   RUUR _L   URRU _A

URDR _N   RUUL _E   URDR _N   LULU _R

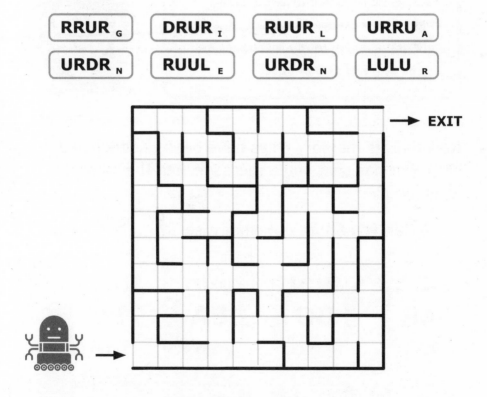

→ EXIT

To exit the maze, our robot has to provide a password. By looking closely at the moves the robot has made, can you work it out?

STEP 14 Chips are down

The robot's memory chips have been scrambled!

a) Can you unjumble these words to fix them?

CLEETILCAR   CHICALEMAN   WRASTOFE

> Each word is a type of engineering that helped create the robot, and I talk about them in my introduction at the start of this chapter.

Now that its memory chips have been unscrambled, the robot has sent you a message. But the message is all jumbled up!

b) Can you figure out what it says?

AR   BO   EA   ME

RO   SO   TS   WE

••••– ––– –••– • •–• ––– • •••– ––– –••– • •–• ––– • •••– ––– –••– • •–• ––– •

FUN FACTS

The gadgets at GCHQ would blow your mind. On the stunning clifftops of North Cornwall is our Bude office, which sits alongside some incredible satellite dishes.

There are twenty-one in total, and these satellite dishes mean we're able to keep up with what's going on in the United Kingdom . . . and the rest of the world!

The smallest satellite dish at Bude stands at 1.2 metres high, which would be a great hiding place for a giant panda, but useless for a giraffe.

The biggest satellite dish is the height of ten double-decker buses piled on top of one another.

STEP 15 On the right track

I want to program our robot to move from the workshop to some of my favourite places. To do this, we need to write instructions for the robot in a way that it can understand. You already have the code for two journeys, which are shown on the map opposite:

Journey 1: From the start to Rose's house
S10; E3; T; S3; B; S4; W2; S3; E1; T; E3; N2; E2

Journey 2: From the start to the train station
S8; W2; S8; E3; S4; B; S5; E2; S3; W4; S4

Can you work out what the code means?

Journey 3: Here is the code for a third journey. Using the map, can you work out what the robot's destination is, if it starts from the robot workshop again?
S4; E5; S4; E3; S5; W1; T; W3; N2; W2; S11; E3; S1; B; S3; E5; T; E3; S4; E2

Journey 4: Here is another code, which doesn't begin at the robot workshop. Where does the robot's journey start and end?
N7; W2; N5; B; N1; E2; N3; E4; B; S3; E6

Journey 5 Can you write the code for a journey from the start to home?

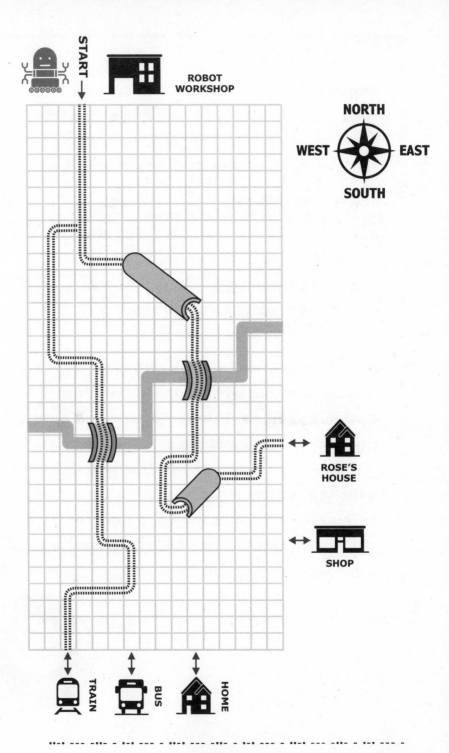

START

ROBOT
WORKSHOP

NORTH
WEST　EAST
SOUTH

ROSE'S
HOUSE

SHOP

TRAIN　BUS　HOME

What you just did is an example of **Reverse Engineering** – the process of finding out how something works. For example, in this puzzle, you have some code that gives instructions to the robot and you want to work out what it does.

You can do this by:

a) Reading the code – this is called **static analysis**. This can be quite difficult, especially when the code is complicated. In this case, you have to think quite carefully about what the letters and numbers might mean.

b) Observing what happens when you run the code, to work out what it does – this is called **dynamic analysis**. This would normally mean building the robot and seeing what it does, but in this puzzle the map shows us what happens when you run the code for Journey 1 and Journey 2. This might help you work out what the letters and numbers mean if you haven't already worked them out from the static analysis.

STEP 16 Power off

Now it's time to shut down the robot for the night. Unfortunately, I've forgotten the shut down code to send it to sleep. I've already tried four different codes, and only have one attempt left!

The good news is that it does tell me if some numbers in part of the code are in the wrong position, or if some numbers are in part of the code and in the correct position.

Can you help me work out the code?

ATTEMPT	GUESS	CORRECT NUMBER IN CORRECT POSITION	CORRECT NUMBER IN WRONG POSITION
1	1234	1	0
2	1567	0	2
3	7296	0	3
4	9674	0	3

Hints

1   Shape 7 is part of image A.

2   The more stars a robot has next to an ability, the better it will be. Because speed is more important than strength, the correct robot must have a higher score (more stars) for speed than for strength.

3   To get you started, look at the robot's legs, and think about what they would look like from the side . . .

4   Shape B 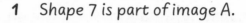 can be made into a cylinder.
The circles are the ends of the cylinder, and the rectangle folds round to make the tube.

5   Sometimes it's easier to decide what something isn't than what it is. Is there a robot that definitely can't be either Ronnie or Romy?

6   Begin by counting the number of each type of piece. Then concentrate next on the rectangles . . .

7   The START cog is turning clockwise. That means the big one next to it will turn anticlockwise, and that makes the next one along turn clockwise. Imagine this cog turning and try to visualise what happens to the cogs next to it.

8   Look at each wire carefully. Are they plugged into the right sockets? Are any wires twisted round another wire?

9 Look at piece H. It has three lines coming in from the right, and none going down. Try to find a piece with three lines coming in from the left, and another piece with no lines going up. These will fit together and you will have nearly completed one board!

10 The building doesn't all need to be finished before the wiring starts. All the wiring is to the body though, so you need to get started with that! The head also takes a long time to build, so perhaps you should get the second team to work on that while the first team is building the body.

11 To get you started, for each combination of Battery and Motor, work out the total weight (and don't forget the weight of the robot itself!).

12 You have to begin by moving A into one of the other slots. Then your only choice is to move B into the other slot. Next you could move A onto B or C, but if you move it onto C then you're a bit stuck . . .

13 The robot has to go right (R) to enter the maze. If it goes right again it would have to go RRRR to keep moving through the maze, and there isn't a move for that. So it must go right and then up (U), and then up again (RUU). Work out which way it has to go next, and you've identified the first move!

14 (a) The answers begin with the letters E, M, S.

(b) The robot is trying to say something about robots, so maybe that's the first word in the message.

15 Look at the compass. What do N, S, E and W mean? The first instruction in Journey 1 is S10, so looking at the map, that must mean moving ten squares in the direction S . . .

16 For the first guess, 1234, the single number which is right is also in the right position. If any of these numbers reappear in guesses where we've been told all the numbers which are correct are in the wrong position (which is the case for the next three guesses), then you know these numbers won't appear in the actual code, so you can eliminate them.

Why not draw your own robot?

Chapter Four

CODEBREAKING

Speaking
in code

Hello, my name is Meg and I work on cryptography research at the National Cyber Security Centre (NCSC), which is part of GCHQ.

Cryptography means the study of codes and includes codebreaking as well as code-making. You can read more about our history in this chapter, where you will find out how GCHQ's team of codebreakers at Bletchley Park helped win the Second World War. Codebreaking isn't just part of our history – some of the work that took place at Bletchley Park is still relevant today, which means it still has to be kept top secret!

With my team, I design the codes that protect the UK's most secret information. To do that, we need to understand how someone might try to break them, so codebreaking is just as important a skill for my role.

I have worked on lots of different types of cryptography – from breaking codes using a pen and paper to researching how cryptography works on a computer. The fun thing about cryptography and breaking codes is that there are so many ways to do it that you never get bored.

Cryptography involves a lot of maths as well as computer skills. When designing codes, I need to think about how I can make them easy enough for the person who will be using them, but tough enough in case someone tries to break them!

The hardest thing about my role is that I need to know about a wide range of topics. It's like when you're at school — you could be doing some maths in the morning, then English lessons, then French. Like me, your brain gets pretty good at jumping from one thing to the next! Are you often tired at the end of the school day? I know how exhausting having to switch between subjects all the time can be!

As a child I loved maths and things like origami — the Japanese art of paper folding, which involves a lot of maths! Have you ever tried origami yourself? When I was younger, I remember making a 3D model of a geometrical shape that I was really proud of.

In this chapter, you'll be using all sorts of skills — maths, languages and being able to spot patterns and shapes — as you learn how to make and break the toughest of codes. You'll need a pencil handy, as codebreaking is all about writing things down, then rubbing them out, then writing things down again as you figure out what a message might mean.

Good luck, puzzlers!

Codebreaking toolkit

Spare pencil

Pencil

Rubber

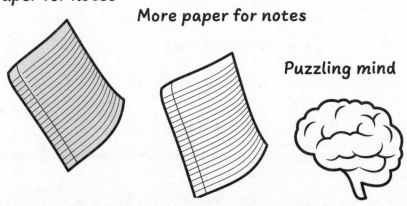

Paper for notes

More paper for notes

Puzzling mind

WHAT IS A CODE?

A code (or a cipher) is a message that has been disguised, so that it can't be read by anyone other than who it was intended for. Codes swap letters, numbers or symbols in place of the components of the original message. The process of turning a message into a code is called encrypting, and the process of taking a code and working out the message is called decrypting.

Normally, the person an encrypted message was intended for will have a way of decrypting the code.

Codebreaking is the process of working out what a message means when you aren't the person it was intended for, and therefore you may not know how it was encrypted! This can sometimes be very difficult, but by the end of this chapter you'll be an expert codemaker and codebreaker.

1 Your first code – as easy as BCD

The simplest types of codes swap each letter in a message with a new letter. For example, you could replace each letter with the next letter on in the alphabet, so **A** would become **B** and so on.

That means if your message is **GCHQ**, then in code it would be encrypted to **HDIR**.

a) Using this rule, decrypt:

MFBSOJOH BCPVU DPEFT JT GVO

Instead of replacing each letter with the next one in the alphabet, you could replace them with a letter that is a different fixed number of letters further on.

For example, if you chose to replace each letter with one that is two letters along in the alphabet, then **A** would encrypt to **C** and so on.

b) Using this rule, decrypt:

ETGCVKPI EQFGU KU HWPPGT!

You could replace each letter with one that is further along the alphabet than two:

c) Can you decrypt this without knowing in advance how far along you need to go?

GWJFPNSL HTIJX NX KZSSJXY!

We can also use numbers to replace letters. For example, you could replace each letter in a message with the number of where it appears in the alphabet. In a code such as this, **A** would become **1**, **B** would become **2** and so on.

d) Using this rule, decrypt:

14.15.23 9.20.19 20.9.13.5

20.15 20.18.25 19.15.13.5

8.1.18.4.5.18 3.15.4.5.19

If you're finding any of these hard, trying writing out the alphabet and counting along.

2 Introducing . . . code blocks

We are now going to show you how to encrypt and decrypt using a **code block**.

Our team of puzzlers has created this method especially for this book! But there are many other ways to encrypt a message.

Here is a simple code block. To create it, we write digits (from 1–9 then 0) followed by the letters of the alphabet in a spiral. Like so:

1	2	3	4	5	6	7	8	9
L	M	N	O	P	Q	R	S	0
K	Z	Y	X	W	V	U	T	A
J	I	H	G	F	E	D	C	B

To use it, we exchange each letter or digit of our message with the letter or digit that is opposite it in the grid, as if the horizontal line in the centre were a mirror.

1	2	3	4	5	6	7	8	9
L	M	N	O	P	Q	R	S	0
K	Z	Y	X	W	V	U	T	A
J	I	H	G	F	E	D	C	B

Imaginary mirror

This means the encryption of V would be Q, and the encryption of H would be 3. Look at the code block above to see how this is done.

If we were to encrypt **GCHQ**, we would get **483V**. And if we were to encrypt **R2D2** we would get **UI7I**.

a) What would you get if you encrypted the word **CODE**?

b) What word is **UX8L6S** the encryption of?

c) What does this encrypted message say?
0 T68U6S Z6TT046

3 Introducing . . . a key

The code block in the previous question could be used by anyone. What if we want to create secret messages in a way that is easy for the person who is receiving the message to read, but harder for others?

Well, we can change the code block.

The way to do this is to use a keyword. We choose a word (say, **DOLPHIN**) and write that into the block first. Then we write all the numbers 1-9 then 0. Finally, we write all the letters that aren't in the keyword after that in alphabetical order. Like so:

A key can be a word or a phrase (or other things!)

D	O	L	P	H	I	N	1	2
F	G	J	K	M	Q	R	S	3
E	Z	Y	X	W	V	U	T	4
C	B	A	0	9	8	7	6	5

a) Now what would you get if you encrypted the word **CODE**?

b) What word is **DBWFS** the encryption of?

c) What does this encrypted message say?
L7BS9FU TFDUFS WFTTLZF

You can even use numbers in your keyword. For example, this is what the code block would look like with the phrase **FAMOUS5**:

F	A	M	O	U	S	5	1	2
H	I	J	K	L	N	P	Q	3
G	Z	Y	X	W	V	T	R	4
E	D	C	B	0	9	8	7	6

As with the letters in the key, we haven't repeated the number 5.

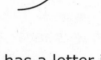

What if the keyword you want to use has a letter in it that's used more than once, like **ELEPHANT**? In this case, you just miss out the repeated letter a second time, so ELEPHANT would become ELPHANT. The code block for ELEPHANT would look like this:

E	L	P	H	A	N	T	1	2
G	I	J	K	M	O	Q	R	3
F	Z	Y	X	W	V	U	S	4
D	C	B	0	9	8	7	6	5

d) Which animal keyword was used to make the below code block?

K	I	L	E	R	W	H	A	1
F	G	J	M	N	O	P	Q	2
D	Z	Y	X	V	U	T	S	3
C	B	0	9	8	7	6	5	4

You should now be able to create your own code blocks using different keywords. Make sure you use a pencil, as it's easy to make mistakes!

e) Complete the code block below for the keyword **VELOCIRAPTOR**.

			O			R		
	F							
B		X					Q	1
0								

Now use it to decrypt the following message:
J9867S9 17 WK43MM56 234U

This system means that you can exchange secret messages with your friends by agreeing to use a keyword that only you (and your friends) know.

We've given you some blank code blocks below so you can try using different keywords to write messages for your friends to decrypt.

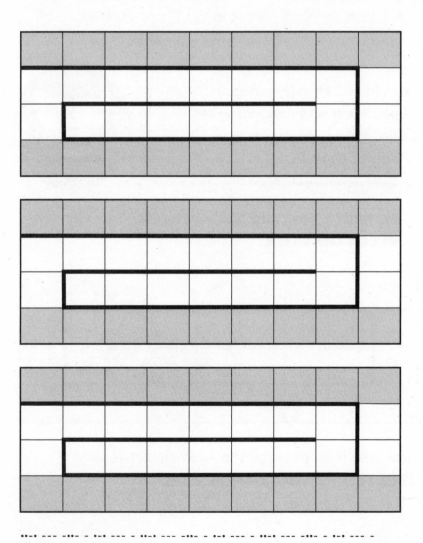

••–• ––– –••– – •–• ––– – ••–• ––– –••– – •–• ––– – ••–• ––– –••– – •–• ––– –

4 Patterns and guesses: cribs and collateral

Sometimes, even if we don't know the code block and keyword being used, we can find patterns in the encrypted letters that enable us to work out what the message says.

We might also have extra information that could help us guess a code. This information is known as **collateral**, and we call our guess a **crib**.

For example, if we knew **XFQQFQQFTTF** was a river, we could work out it was **MISSISSIPPI**, because of the various double letters, and we know each letter encrypts to the same letter each time.

>   **a)** The following item was found on an
>   encrypted shopping list: **3C7C7C**.
>   What word has been encrypted?
>
>   **b)** What planet is **7DL0J7D**?

THE STORY OF GCHQ:
The Enigma machine

When it comes to code-breaking, some incredible machines have been created to help us decrypt the toughest messages.

During the Second World War, we needed to understand secret messages sent by German soldiers and spies. They were using a machine called Enigma, which was originally built for German banks to make their messages as secret as possible.

The Germans thought their Enigma messages were unbreakable. The Enigma machine ensured each message they wrote was coded in a slightly different way, and the number of codes the machine could make was astronomical. There were 3,283,883,513,7 96,974,198,700,882,069,882,752,878,379,955,261,0 95,623,685,444,055,315,226,006,433,615,627,409,66 6,933,182,371,154,802,769,920,000,000,000 possible combinations of a three-rotor Enigma. What made it even tougher was that the combination changed every day!

But decoding the message was made possible by some very clever Polish mathematicians, working with codebreakers in the United Kingdom, including Alan Turing and Gordon Welchman.

The only way Enigma could be broken was to create a different machine, so Turing and Welchman designed something that became known as the BOMBE, to help them figure it out.

Each BOMBE machine was about 2 metres wide and 2 metres tall and weighed almost a tonne. It had nearly 12 miles of wire inside it. By the end of the war, over 200 of them had been built.

The work to understand the Enigma and other enemy cipher machines helped shorten the Second World War, and saved hundreds of thousands of lives.

— The Enigma machine

5 One and the same

A clever thing about code blocks is that the process of encrypting and decrypting is the same. This means that if – for example – **A** encrypts to **P**, then **P** encrypts to **A**. Using this, answer the following questions.

> A different code block is used for each question, but you don't need to make them – you should be able to find the answers out without them!

a) If **ELFIA** is **LEMON** what is **EOFL**?

b) What month is **UR7JRA1**?

c) What colour of the rainbow is **GARWOB**?

d) You intercept the following message between Alice and Bob, encrypted using an unknown code block. You think the fifth word might be **CODE**. See if you can use this to decrypt the rest of the message:

YP CLFNHM SFDDNUBSRGP BU SFMP CF GLRG UFIFMW SRU APRM FNA DPCCRTPC

6 The Enigma method

What would happen if we changed the code block for every letter? We don't have enough information to make each code block, and we can't use the letter pattern technique from puzzle 4. But we do know that one feature of code blocks is that they never encrypt a letter to itself. This means that the letter P will never encrypt to the letter P!

Given this, can you answer the following:

a) Is **TVXQR** the encryption of **HEADS** or **TAILS**?

b) What day of the week is **MUFXLP**?

c) Which sign of the zodiac is **QAGEWS**?

d) What number is **PVN**, if you know it's greater than **QEVL**?

7 Reconstructing a code block

For these questions, you will need to reconstruct a code block to work out each message. We've given you blank code blocks to fill in.

a) One day, I received the following message, encrypted using the keyword **MEERKAT**:

FVWE0J 19G MDKCP0CJ WV9GZWH 9V CDUVC9

What did the message say?

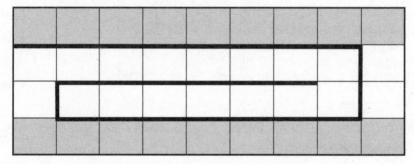

b) The next day, the same person sent the following message, using a new keyword:
0MFNWCJ H09 EFRBMCBJ S809ZS7 08 BFQ8B0

Can you guess what the message says, without decrypting it?

c) Now find the keyword.

In order to find the new keyword you need to reconstruct the code block that was used. Begin by writing out all the known decode/encode pairs from your decryption of the message in part b). Remember that they decode to each other – for example, if I encodes to Z then Z encodes to I.

In the block below you can see where Y and Z normally sit. Find which letters they encode/decode to, and put them in the block.

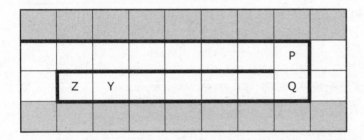

Finding encode/decode pairs in which the two letters are adjacent in the alphabet can help. Although they have to be opposite each other in the code block, they will likely also be next to each other in the spiral!

See where the pair P and Q go. What other such pair do you have? Where in the code block can they go? Can you now deduce two letters that must be in the keyword as they are missing from the alphabetical section? Now you have a start, look to see what the digits encode/ decode to. This may help with the keyword. Hakuna Matata!

PEOPLE FROM OUR PAST

NAME:
Mavis Batey

ROLE:
Mathematician
and codebreaker

FACT:
Mavis was eagle-eyed. During the Second World War, she broke a top secret message that showed the Italian navy was preparing for battle.

DID YOU KNOW?
Her codebreaking on certain types of Enigma was groundbreaking, so she wrote a guide on how to do it for future codebreakers.

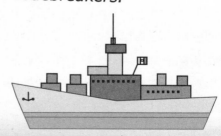

FUN FACTS

GCHQ's archives are a treasure-trove of secrets. The rows and rows of shelving contain 16 million documents from hundreds of years of history. These documents tell incredible stories and give us a glimpse into how the early codebreakers went about their work.

In order not to be wasteful, Bletchley Park codebreakers used to turn their pads of notes (from writing down secret messages) into top secret paper decorations for the Christmas tree!

Some of the 1,800 artefacts and items in our archives are even older than GCHQ itself. There are stories of spies and codebooks from as long ago as 1809!

8 Puzzling polygons

Using the key phrase **CIPHERS AND CODES**, decrypt the following:

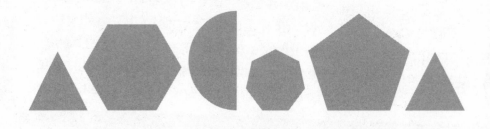

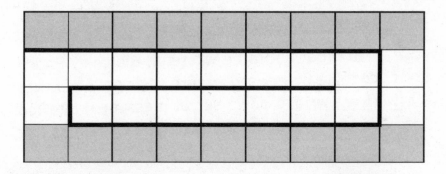

Check the hint on page 137 if you get stuck.

9 Catch of the day

Mavis and her fellow codebreakers – working away in the Cottage at Bletchley Park – had fun names to describe the techniques they used to break messages encrypted by the Enigma machine.

Codebreaking is all about finding patterns in encrypted messages, and Mavis would call these patterns **lobsters** or **crabs**.

Lobsters and crabs look like this:

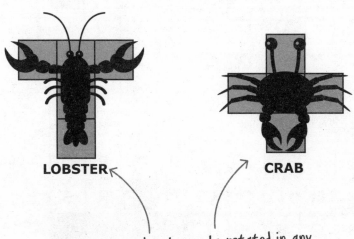

LOBSTER

CRAB

The lobsters and crabs can be rotated in any direction (as you can see on the next page).

For this puzzle, lobsters and crabs are made up of five grid squares containing five consecutive letters of the alphabet (in any order).

In the grid below, a lobster (containing the letters I, J, K, L and M) and a crab (containing the letters E, F, G, H and I) have been shaded in.

Can you hunt down the remaining lobsters and crabs hidden in the grid, shading them in as you go?

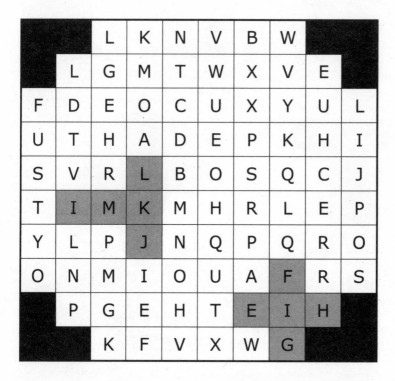

The unshaded letters will spell out something that should be familiar. What is it?

10 Bletchley Park – Hut 8

During the Second World War, the codebreakers in Hut 8 at Bletchley Park were responsible for decrypting messages sent at sea.

The deadly U-boats – German submarines – would send messages to each other that would be intercepted and sent to Bletchley Park for decrypting.

On the next page, we have been given a map of U-boat sightings and the signals they're transmitting. Unfortunately, the overlapping transmissions make these difficult to read, so you need to figure them out.

Each U-boat is transmitting a word from the NATO phonetic alphabet in which each letter of the alphabet is assigned to a particular word. ALFA is 'a', BRAVO is 'b', and so on . . . We've given you the alphabet at the end of the question.

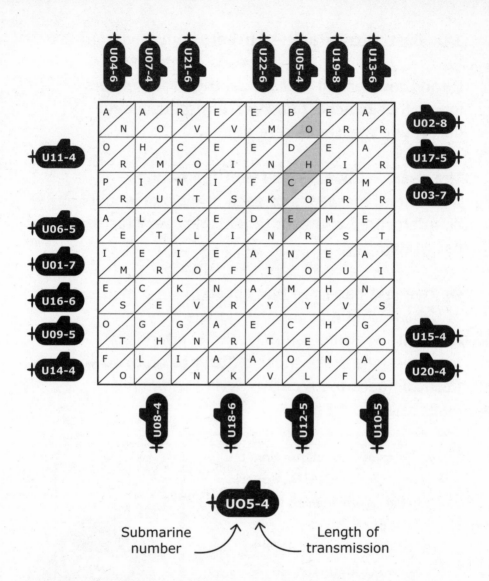

Submarine number ← → Length of transmission

The length of transmission shows you how many letters are in the phonetic word. The first letter of each phonetic word will appear furthest from the submarine, and will run in the direction going back towards it, as shown in the example: ECHO.

The initial letters from each word come together to form a message. The submarine number tells you where the letter should be placed in the message (the letter E from ECHO has been placed for you).

$$\underset{1}{\rule{2em}{0.4pt}} \quad \underset{2}{\rule{2em}{0.4pt}} \quad \underset{3}{\rule{2em}{0.4pt}} \quad \underset{4}{\rule{2em}{0.4pt}} \quad \overset{\text{E}}{\underset{5}{\rule{2em}{0.4pt}}} \quad \underset{6}{\rule{2em}{0.4pt}}$$

| 7 | 8 | 9 | 10 | 11 | 12 | 13 |

| 14 | 15 | 16 |

| 17 | 18 |

| 19 | 20 | 21 | 22 |

Can you find the secret message, and figure out what word it reveals?

A – ALFA	J – JULIETT	S – SIERRA
B – BRAVO	K – KILO	T – TANGO
C – CHARLIE	L – LIMA	U – UNIFORM
D – DELTA	M - MIKE	V – VICTOR
E – ECHO	N – NOVEMBER	W – WHISKEY
F – FOXTROT	O – OSCAR	X – X-RAY
G – GOLF	P – PAPA	Y – YANKEE
H – HOTEL	Q – QUEBEC	Z - ZULU
I – INDIA	R – ROMEO	

Some letters will be in twice, and some won't be used at all.

.... --- ---- - .-. --- - .... --- ---- - .-. --- - .... --- ---- - .-. --- -

Hints

1 We'll give you the first word for question **a)** MFBSOJOH, when decrypted, becomes LEARNING.

2 If you're finding question **c)** tricky, try working out one letter at a time. You can see that T is a mirror of S in the code block, 6 is a mirror of E and 8 a mirror of C. So the second word must begin SEC . . .

3 Remember you shouldn't be repeating any letters in your code block! The animal in the code block for question **d)** is a type of whale . . .

4 Think about what you might find on a shopping list – maybe fruit? Can you think of a fruit where every other letter is the same?

5 See if you can crack question **b)** by looking carefully at the months in the year and seeing if you can match any patterns in the encrypted word to the months themselves. You're looking for a month with seven letters, and where the second and fifth letter are the same . . .

6 For question **b)**, you know the day of the week must be six letters, so that narrows it down to three days. Now remember that a letter can't encrypt to itself . . .

7 Often in codebreaking we have to make educated guesses! The second message is exactly the same number of letters as the first one, except for the first word, so it's likely to be very similar. Given that this message was received the next day, what do you think it could be?

For part **c)** the keyword is an animal whose name is the same length as the one in part **a)**, but with all its letters different. Use this fact to put the digits 1 to 9 and 0 into the blank code block, and write in what they decode/encode to.

8 Try counting the sides of each shape.

9 Here are a few more lobsters and crabs:.

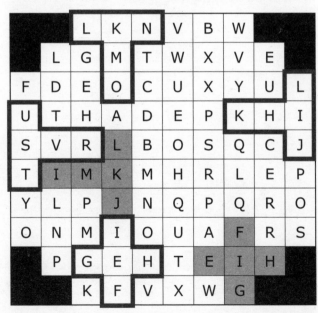

10 UO1–7 is where you'll find your UNIFORM.

Chapter Five

ANALYSIS

A needle
in a haystack

Hey, everyone! My name is Riley. I'm an analyst working at our office in Bude, Cornwall. The office is on a clifftop, overlooking the coast. When some of my colleagues aren't working, you might find them surfing!

Being an analyst is all about solving problems. My work is a bit like finding the missing pieces of a jigsaw and slotting them together, so you have the complete picture. We need to check a lot of different places to find different pieces of information and put it all together to work out what it means.

Analysis could, for example, help uncover criminal activity, so the police can stop them, or find a person who's been kidnapped. We might do this by piecing together information about a crime from data gathered across the internet, so we can then use it to help trace the person or people who committed the crime.

Everything we do has to be legal, and gathering information from people is done only when it is completely necessary. We always have to get special permission from the right people before we carry out any operations like this.

Before joining GCHQ, I was trying to choose between a job doing technical stuff (what I do now!) or a more creative job, like animation for films. Even though analysis is definitely technical (lots of computers and maths), I find being creative helps me to think differently about certain problems, which I can then discuss with my fellow workers. I love working as a team in this way!

The main thing I love about working at GCHQ is that I'm part of a mission that matters. We all work together to keep the country safe. And, because technology is always changing, GCHQ must keep inventing new ways of working so we can stay ahead. That's a really exciting thing to be a part of.

A lot of my job is a bit like having to find a really small needle in a massive haystack, and practising solving puzzles is crucial to that.

In this chapter, we'll need your best puzzling skills! You're going to be teaming up with me to focus on a case looking at five suspects who we think might all be be up to no good (and you can find out exactly what on page 257 of this book!). We need to find out as much about them as possible, and the following puzzles all contain clues to their whereabouts and communications.

Some are a bit tough. But analysis is all about looking for patterns where there seemingly aren't any, so you can put that jigsaw together. If you get stuck, have a look at those hints on page 164.

Good luck – we're counting on you!

MISSION BRIEFING:

. . . .

Your mission has arrived . . .

Our five suspects have worked hard to hide their identities, so we need to refer to them as A, B, C, D and E.

We've gathered information on each suspect to help us find out more about them so we can work out what they're up to and who is in charge. But a lot of it is jumbled up, or hard to understand.

You need to look closely at all the information and answer the questions to crack this case!

MATHS

Elizabeth

We have found a mysterious set of numbers, sent from the group leader, which we believe reveals the number of the vault in which can be found the deposit box containing the laptop. Once we know the number we can open the vault and look for it.

These puzzles form part of the Team Challenge, which starts on p257.

Colour in the grid so that each square is red, yellow, green or blue. Each number and arrow tells you how many squares there are along the rest of that row or column that are **the same colour as the NUMBER:**

	3↓	1←	2↓		2→			3↓
			3→		2→			
1↑	1↑			1←			1↓	
2↓	2↓	2↑		2↑		2↑		1↓
	3↑		2↑			1↓	1←	
		2↑		3↑	4↑		1↓	1↓
	2→		2↑	3←	2→			

Once you have coloured in the grid, can you trace the orange path to recover the secret number?

Shanti

The vault has so many deposit boxes that ONLY A ROBOT could reach so high! But our robot has been sabotaged. Can you put it back together?

Reassemble the robot so that the colours match this picture.

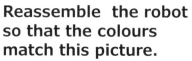

The pieces need to be laid on top of each other to create the robot. In what order do they need to be laid, from top to bottom?

ANALYSIS

Riley

Even when we have access to the laptop we still need to know the STOP CODE. The table below was found underneath the leader's snooker table, and was used to create codes. GCHQ knows the last sixteen codes used, and we know the next one in the list is the one we need. But what is it?

J	Y	X	H	P	M	G	J	Q	K	D	U
M	U	Z	B	H	V	J	S	C	Q	G	N
I	J	U	Q	O	L	F	B	K	P	Y	E
W	S	V	X	A	G	T	C	Z	B	M	D
C	L	W	Y	N	S	R	E	G	A	H	O
O	Z	F	D	R	J	I	N	W	M	E	H
P	V	J	R	T	E	K	D	S	U	W	G
H	B	L	Z	I	A	U	V	E	W	F	R
F	A	O	U	S	I	Y	L	B	R	X	W
U	W	K	J	M	C	A	O	I	L	T	Y
G	X	E	M	Y	W	Q	I	N	C	P	L
K	R	S	T	F	N	D	X	U	O	Z	V

GAKTPI, RBGCGO
IZWYYV, YXNMTY

JULDFE, JCKBMG
KXXJNM, QLSWXU

CBFBOL, DIUAFN
FYOMTW, INZRYW

MJEXAJ, TDCLDH
PVVZIN, UEEPWV

??????

CITY GRID CHALLENGE

	T	H				X	
		C	D	U	M		
	I		I	M		T	
	O	G			Y	U	
	E	R			S	D	
	C			L		O	
		O		D	R		

2 digit square

For you

Digits which sum to 15

5!

3 consecutive digits

____ Humbug

Fish

Disney Elephant

Intelligence Agency

Disney Parrot

Frozen water

Pound

Month

Healthcare system

Star Wars Robot

Sprint

A star

____ Friday's

90

1 Look who's talking

We've discovered that each of the suspects uses a different piece of technology to communicate with the others. I've got a note giving us some clues, but it's jumbled up.

Can you unscramble it?

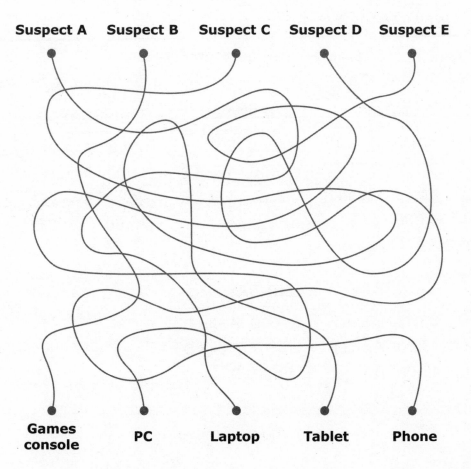

2 Notebook clues

We've discovered a notebook with a list of letters and numbers inside, and have worked out that this is a record of the times that Suspect C has met with the other suspects.

We believe the suspect they have met most often is the person they are working with most closely. Which suspect is this?

MONDAY:

10:00	E
11:00	D
14:00	A and B
19:00	B

TUESDAY:

09:00	D
10:00	A and E
18:00	B and E

THURSDAY:

09:00	A and D
13:00	A and E
13:30	B and E
20:00	A and E

SATURDAY:

09:15	B and E
13:00	A and E
19:00	A

SUNDAY:

09:00	B and D
14:30	B and D
19:00	D

3 Spinning a web

Using information gathered by my team, I've created a diagram of a number of people – including our suspects – travelling from a meeting place.

It also includes the time in minutes it took to make each journey.

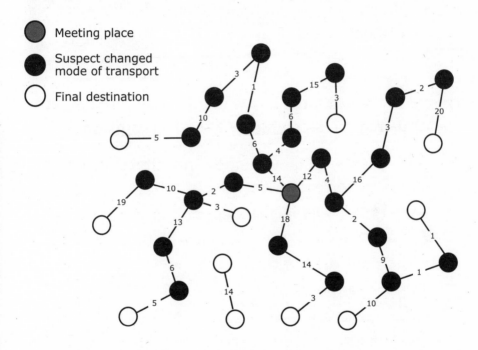

Meeting place

Suspect changed mode of transport

Final destination

a) We know Suspect D took 39 minutes to reach their final destination. Can you work out which route they took?

b) We also know that Suspect A took over 40 minutes to reach their final location. How many different routes could they have taken?

4 The magic number

We have a list of possible phone numbers for Suspect B, and need to work out which is theirs.

We know that a phone number can open the door to a lot of important clues.

One of my teammates has worked through the night to uncover some facts, so we already know:

- They have a phone number from the UK, which means it starts with +44.
- When the +44 is included, phone numbers from the UK are twelve digits long.
- The third digit of the phone number is 7.
- Phone numbers should only include digits.
- Somewhere in their phone number there is a 3.

Looking at the list opposite, can you work out which is Suspect B's phone number?

1. +447700900000

2. +447700907

3. +327761895456

4. +447700901525459

5. +44c7700907

6. +447700901729968532

7. 903b510d5622a93d38671e5b1f1ca4b6

8. +447700900172997

9. +447700901396

10. +4477009001729973186

11. +447700900717

12. +4477009001749091

13. +4477009017494h64308

5 Lock and key

We have recovered a note that Suspect A uses to remember their code to a safe, but some of the numbers are missing.

Each of the numbers from 0 to 9 must be used once. Can you spot the pattern and work out which digits should replace the question marks?

$$8 - 5 - ? - 9 - ? - ? - 6 - ? - 2 - 0$$

FUN FACTS

Our people work around the clock, including Christmas Day and bank holidays. So, whatever time it is, the lights of GCHQ are always on, and teams are hard at work helping to keep the UK and our allies safe.

HRH The Duke of Cambridge (Prince William) has spent time working with our shiftteams. His father, the Prince of Wales, is the patron of the Intelligence Services – which includes GCHQ, MI5 and MI6.

We're a superstitious lot. The Q word (quiet) is banned in our 24/7 operations centre as we don't want to tempt fate. Teams finishing the night shift or starting the morning shift will often treat themselves to a breakfast cooked in our restaurant.

6 Profile puzzle

Some information has come to light about ten people. Can you help us work out which five of them are our suspects?

> *Our potential suspects are labelled from **a** to **j**, but it could be any of them!*

We know one thing about each of them, and one thing about all of them:

- One of our suspects has a twin; his twin sister is also on the list but is not a suspect.

- One plays basketball, and benefits from being very tall.

- One supports the Welsh rugby team because of their birthplace.

- One is proud of his Yorkshire roots.

- One is less than 5 foot 3 inches tall.

- All of them left school at least five years ago.

	AGE	PLACE OF BIRTH	HEIGHT (CM)	MALE/FEMALE
a	32	London	165	M
b	29	Belfast	199	M
c	57	Guildford	180	M
d	45	York	162	F
e	29	Swansea	173	F
f	32	London	164	F
g	60	Dundee	158	F
h	18	Bristol	153	F
i	35	London	171	M
j	28	Leeds	161	M

7 Work patterns

We've gathered some data on Suspect B that shows the time and date of when they entered and exited their place of work during three weeks in March.

CLOCKING-IN AND -OUT TIMES

Monday 7th March
08:14 → 16:31

Tuesday 8th March
08:12 → 16:33

Wednesday 9th March
08:07 → 18:04

Thursday 10th March
08:05 → 16:34

Friday 11th March
08:09 → 16:46

Monday 14th March
08:45 → 17:01

Tuesday 15th March
08:02 → 11:35
12:01 → 17:02

Wednesday 16th March
08:32 → 17:01

Friday 18th March
07:22 → 17:06

Monday 21st March
08:06 → 17:04

Tuesday 22nd March
08:05 → 17:05

Wednesday 23rd March
08:11 → 17:01

Thursday 24th March
08:03 → 17:06

Friday 25th March
08:10 → 17:09

a) Suspect B is expected to be at work Monday to Friday each week. What day didn't they turn up when they were meant to?

b) Suspect B tends to always have lunch at the office. Did they leave the office at any point during the period in question?

c) We're aware that, like their colleagues, Suspect B is allowed to be in the office between 8 a.m. and 5.30 p.m. Did Suspect B ever attend the office outside these times?

d) We believe that Suspect B may have stolen a document from a safe in the office. It would take them at least 35 minutes alone in the office to crack the safe. Which date and between what times did the theft take place?

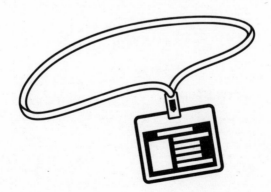

THE STORY OF GCHQ:
Stuck in traffic

Some people refer to GCHQ as a signals intelligence agency. This means that intelligence is gathered by intercepting and reading communications. One thing we use is **Traffic Analysis**. This means that we try to understand how people of interest use, say, their phones to pass messages to each other. Once we can understand that it makes it easier to get hold of the signals and find out what they're saying.

During the Second World War, traffic analysis was very important, and at Bletchley Park a whole section was created to pull it all together in Hut 6.

There were many different huts at Bletchley Park, and they were often painted green. The experts in Hut 6 were busy creating new machines so they could break the codes which had been found using

Traffic Analysis. But there was also a special hut set aside for games and relaxing.

We remember the work done at Bletchley Park in lots of different ways. Today, some of our most important top secret missions are even done in rooms that we still call huts. The people in these huts work night and day to crack cases – proof that GCHQ never stops!

Hard at work in Hut 6 at Bletchley Park.

8 Botanical brainteaser

We have been alerted to an important discovery!

This page is torn from an encyclopaedia that was found along with part of a plane ticket. But the cities the suspect is flying to are missing, and we need to figure out where they're going.

BOARDING P

Flight number: 3122175

> > > > > > > > > > > >

> > > > > > > > > > > >

Broccoli (*Brassica oleracea var. italica*) is an edible green plant in the cabbage family (family Brassicaceae, genus Brassica) whose large flowering head, stalk and small associated leaves are eaten as a vegetable. Broccoli is classified in the Italica cultivar group of the species Brassica oleracea. Broccoli has large flower heads, usually dark green, arranged in a tree-like structure branching out from a thick stalk which is usually light green. The mass of flower heads is surrounded by leaves. Broccoli resembles cauliflower, which is a different but closely related cultivar group of the same Brassica species.

It appears that Suspect D has scribbled some text below the article:

7,1; 3,35; 11,11; 8,11; 4,7; 1,38

Then on to:

(6,30; 12,3; 2,7; 9,16; 5,22; 13,13) R

Can you make sense of this? Where is Suspect D going?

·-·· ·· -- ·- ·-·· ·· -- ·- ·-·· ·· -- ·- ·-·· ·· -- ·- ·-·· ·· -- ·-

9 Briefcase password

We have found a slip of paper that dropped out of Suspect E's briefcase. It looks like there is a password hidden within a grid of letters. There is a key at the top of the page to help Suspect E remember their password.

The letters in the key correspond to a letter in the password. In the grid below, the password letter will be to the left, right, above or below the key letters.

We also know that the password is a real, complete word. Can you find out what it is?

Q	X	Y	M	O	R	H

Q	T	S	I	C	E	E	L
A	L	Y	V	K	I	O	B
N	U	W	A	J	U	Z	J
D	S	K	T	P	C	G	F
S	X	J	B	M	T	W	G
N	E	I	Z	N	P	D	N
P	A	G	H	K	F	U	R
B	D	L	N	Z	V	W	C

10 Phone call conundrum

We have intercepted a phone call made to Suspect E, but we need to work out which suspect was making the call.

This was the phone call:

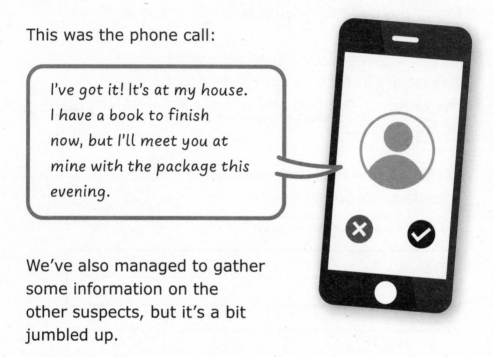

> I've got it! It's at my house. I have a book to finish now, but I'll meet you at mine with the package this evening.

We've also managed to gather some information on the other suspects, but it's a bit jumbled up.

What is clear though is that the four other suspects – A, B, C and D – live in four different places. We also know that each of them speaks one foreign language, and what their jobs are.

Can you look at the information opposite and work out who was making the call?

- There is a suspect who lives in Manchester. A second suspect speaks Italian, and a third suspect is an engineer. None of these is Suspect A.

- Suspect C and Suspect D cannot speak French.

- Suspect C lives south of Suspect A and north of Suspect D.

- The author speaks Swedish.

- The teacher lives in Scarborough.

- The one who lives in Cheltenham speaks German.

- The banker does not live in Manchester.

- Suspect B lives in London.

- The teacher and the banker do not speak German.

- The French speaker does not live in London.

11 Needle in a haystack

We have intercepted a letter to Suspect D.

We believe it contains the location of where they are heading next. Can you solve it?

FROG   LION   TOAD

CENTAUR   DOG

SLOTH   HEN

5: ignore space

12 Which receipt?

We have shop receipts from all five of our suspects. Each receipt has a crucial bit of information, but we need to link the right receipt to the right suspect.

We know all the suspects live alone so won't be buying things for anyone else. Only A, C and D are known to have pets. We also know:

- A doesn't like fizzy drinks.
- B and C are vegetarian and so don't eat meat or fish.
- E has a nut allergy, so can't eat any sort of nut in any food.
- B, D and E chew gum – the rest don't.

Here are the receipts. Can you work out which receipt is for which suspect?

1
vegetarian sausages
tomatoes
mushrooms
carrots
toothpaste

2
newspaper
Snickers bar
shampoo
potatoes
cola

3
tissues
eggs
bacon
tomato ketchup
dog toy

4
bread
2 tins of beans
bubblegum
bag of peanuts
magazine

5
cheese
chewing gum
vegetarian burger mix
goldfish food
flowers

13 Follow the leader

We've discovered a new suspect: Suspect F.

We have seen messages between some of our suspects and Suspect F, and are trying to work out if Suspect F is the person directly in charge of the group.

Over the last twenty-four hours we have intercepted messages being sent between individuals, and you can see below who was speaking to who.

Do you think F is in charge? If not, who might be?

F → A, A → F, F → B, D → F, C → E, F → D,

E → C, A → B, B → F, E → C, A → B, C → E,

F → A, F → B, B → F, C → E, B → F, E → C,

A → B, D → C, D → B, D → E, E → C, D → A,

A → D, D → A, D → F, A → B, B → F, C → E,

C → D, E → D, B → D, A → D, B → A, F → D,

F → B, B → A, A → F, E → C

Check page 257 to find the next challenge involving our suspects!

PEOPLE FROM OUR PAST

NAME:

Margaret Rock

ROLE:

Analyst, codebreaker and linguist

FACT:

Margaret's work analysing German messages massively impressed Dilly Knox, who had this to say about her:

Miss Rock is entirely in the wrong grade. She is actually fourth or fifth best of the whole Enigma staff and quite as useful as some of the 'professors'. I recommend that she should be put on the highest possible salary for anyone of her seniority.

DID YOU KNOW?

In letters published to her brother John in the book Dear Codebreaker, Margaret could not talk about her top secret work. Instead, she wrote about her experiences in the London Blitz.

Hints

1 Try carefully following the lines from each suspect, and see where they lead.

2 Count the number of times each letter occurs in the notebook . . .

3 You can work out the journey times taken by adding up the numbers along each route.

4 Try narrowing down the numbers using the information you have. Maybe find the numbers with twelve digits to start off with.

5 Try writing each number out as a word, and look at the first letter of each number. Does it help you spot the pattern?

6 Start by seeing if you can rule any of the suspects out. For instance, you know that **h** can't be a suspect, as they must have left school very recently.

7 Look carefully at the times you've been given. The ones early in the morning must be when the suspect entered work, and the ones late afternoon when they left. These tend to be close to 08:00 and 17:00. So, when attempting the questions, see if you can find times that differ significantly from these . . .

8 The solution lies in the number of lines in the passage, and the number of letters along each line.

·—·· ·· —— ·— ·—··· ·· —— ·— ·—·· ·· —— ·— ·—··· ·· —— ·—

9 Try out different combinations of letters, and see if you can spot a word emerging . . .

10 Start by thinking about what type of person you're looking for. In what job would someone be writing a book? Then, if you're struggling to find who has that job, try filling in as much information about each suspect as possible. For instance, you know that Suspect B lives in London, and the others must live in Cheltenham, Scarborough or Manchester. Using a map of the United Kingdom, can the third clue help you find out who lives where?

11 Try counting along the letters of the message.

12 Don't make assumptions – just because someone isn't stated as being vegetarian, doesn't mean they won't buy vegetarian food. We also know three suspects chew gum, but only two receipts have chewing gum or bubblegum on them. Try starting with receipt 5. This should belong to someone who chews gum and owns a pet – does anyone fit this description? Then try seeing if you can work out the receipt with the other gum on it.

13 See if you can find the suspect who talks to everyone else in the group, as they're likely to be the person in charge. Drawing a diagram, with arrows, to show who speaks to who might help with this.

Chapter Six

MATHEMATICS

A journey through numbers

Hi puzzlers, my name is Elizabeth. I work in mathematics and data science at GCHQ's Manchester office.

After studying maths at university, I started to teach it in schools. I had heard a lecture at university by a GCHQ mathematician and their work seemed important (but really fun!), so I applied online and began working there.

GCHQ mathematicians work on all sorts of things, from data science to signals analysis. We use maths to make sure technology is safe. Maths ultimately helps us solve difficult problems.

For example, we write complicated algorithms so computers work as well as possible and are as safe as they can be. An algorithm is basically a list of clear instructions that a person (or computer) can follow to achieve an intended result. You could think of it as being a bit like a recipe you might follow to cook a specific meal.

Some of the maths I use in my job is similar to the stuff I learned at school and university, but I also had

a lot of training when I first joined. Not everyone will learn the same elements of maths as they grow up, so we have training to make sure we all have the same level of knowledge. Learning never stops here though! I still go on courses, read books and watch videos, and pick up things from my fellow workers too, of course.

Since joining GCHQ, I've done some really cool things. I'm currently working in data science, where I'm developing an algorithm that we hope to use to identify evidence of a cyber attack on a computer network, so then other people at GCHQ can take action to stop it. You can read more about cyber from my colleague Sandeep in the Cyber Security chapter on page 228.

I find it really rewarding to see how my work helps keep people in the UK safe. But one of my favourite things about working for GCHQ is that there are so many people here who like maths. In our spare time, lots of us enjoy playing games together and solving puzzles. It's great to work somewhere where you can meet new friends with similar interests to your own. Outside work, I'm also part of a local choir and an active member of a local church too.

A good mathematician spends time figuring out how things work and, when they get something wrong, takes this as an opportunity to keep thinking and learning. With maths, there is often a right answer, but it isn't always easy to find straight away. It's good to puzzle it through to work it out (and doing this with other people really helps!).

In this chapter, we'll be taking a tour through the history of mathematics together. We'll see what different number systems have been used in the past, and where the maths that we work on at GCHQ came from.

Good luck, and happy puzzling.

1 The foundations of mathematics

Mathematics is built on very solid foundations. It'd be a shame if it all came tumbling down!

Can you rebuild the wall by placing the bricks back into their correct positions, so that each row spells out a connected group of mathematical words?

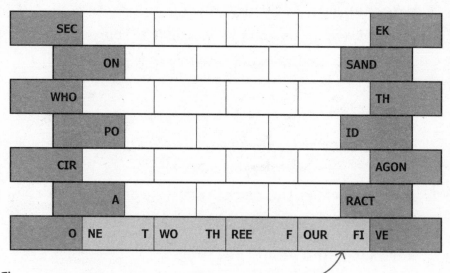

SEC					EK
ON			SAND		
WHO				TH	
PO			ID		
CIR				AGON	
A			RACT		
O	NE	T	WO	TH	REE	F	OUR	FI	VE

The bottom row has been completed for you.

APE	SOL	ARE	PENT	AY	WE	CENT	TRIA	CLE	CRES
DD	DIV	DRED	THOU	E	TE	IDE	MULT	INT	LI
IPLY	SUBT	IRD	QUAR	LE	HA	LF	TH	N	HUN
NE	SH	NE	T	NGLE	SQU	OND	MIN	OUR	FI
REE	F	TER	FIF	UR	D	UTE	HO	WO	TH

2 Six-in-one

Write a whole number between 0 and 9 in each empty square in the diagram below, so that the sums above the arrows pointing between the two squares are correct.

The dashed lines don't tell you anything – so really this is six puzzles in one question!

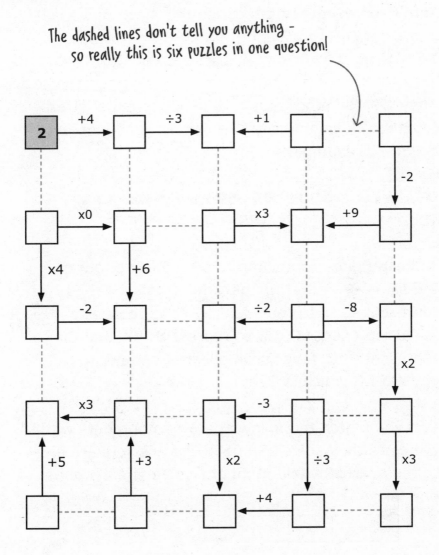

3 What the Romans did for us

Over two thousand years ago, the Romans came up with a system of writing numbers using the letters I, V, X, L, C, D and M.

These represented numbers:

I=1, V=5, X=10, L=50, C=100, D=500, M=1,000

They created other numbers by putting the letters together, beginning with the largest, and working down. For example:

DCLXVIII is **500+100+50+10+5+1+1+1**.
This means that it is **668**.

To keep things short, and to save writing four of the same symbols together, the Romans used IV to represent 4, IX to represent 9, XL to represent 40, XC to represent 90, CD to represent 400 and CM to represent 900. A very complicated number therefore is CMXCIX, which is 999.

Can you match the following Roman numbers with the clues they solve? Some of the answers are given to the nearest whole number (we've already done one for you).

MDCIX	days in a year?
CCCV	metres in a mile?
DCCXXX	seconds in an hour?
MMMDC	millimetres in a foot?
CLXVIII	minutes in a day?
CCCLXV	yards in a kilometre?
XXXIX	hours in a week?
MXCIV	inches in a metre?
MCDXL	average hours in a month?

Now can you find these Roman numbers in the number-search below? Once you've found them all, the remaining letters will spell out in Roman numbers the year that GCHQ was formed. Which year was that?

X	X	X	I	X	I
V	X	M	C	M	I
L	X	X	V	X	I
X	C	L	I	I	V
D	C	C	C	V	X
C	D	X	X	C	L
M	M	M	M	D	C

Later, the Arabic numbers 0, 1, 2 through to 9 were invented, and have now become the most common way to write numbers.

4 Game, Set, Matchstick

With the Arabic number system, we can use numbers that Romans had no way of writing – such as zero and numbers less than zero!

You can form the digits 0 to 9 using matchsticks:

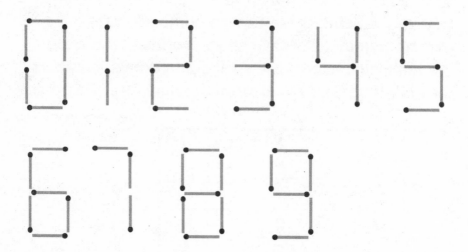

You can use these matchstick versions to create puzzles! In each of the puzzles opposite, you are presented with a sum that is wrong.

You have to move **one** matchstick to make the sum correct, and you cannot remove any of the matchsticks. Which one and where do you move it?

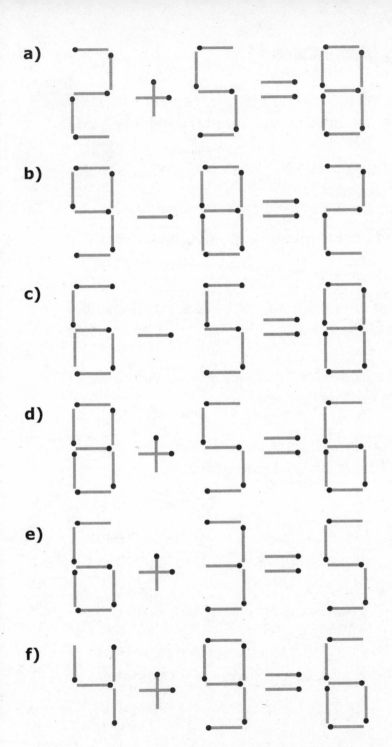

a) 2 + 5 = 8

b) 9 - 8 = 2

c) 6 - 5 = 8

d) 8 + 5 = 6

e) 6 + 3 = 5

f) 4 + 9 = 6

5 Filling in the Caps

When you write down numbers or capital letters, you sometimes use both straight and curved lines, and sometimes just straight lines. Also, some capital letters and numbers have enclosed spaces and some don't. For example:

A is formed only from straight lines, and it has an enclosed space.

M is formed only from straight lines, but doesn't have an enclosed space.

R is formed from straight lines and curved lines, and has an enclosed space.

5 is formed from straight lines and curved lines, but doesn't have an enclosed space.

a) The word NINETY-FIVE uses only straight lines when written as a word in capital letters.

The number 417 uses only straight lines when written in digits.

Which number uses only straight lines when written in digits and as a word?

b) The word TWENTY-FIVE has no enclosed spaces when written as a word in capital letters.

The number 25 also has no enclosed spaces when written as a number.

What is the smallest number that has both these properties? So, no enclosed spaces when written as a word or as a number?

c) What is the largest number that has both the properties in part b?

6 Elevenses

When we write numbers as words, we can count the letters in those words, and get more numbers!

For example, 700 can be written as SEVEN HUNDRED, which is **twelve** letters long.

Bearing this in mind, can you figure out what this sequence represents and work out what comes next?

1, 4, 3, 11, 15, 13, 17, 24, ?

7 Letters and numbers

In the tenth century, the Persian mathematician Al-Karaji showed how we could use letters to represent numbers, paving the way for what we now call algebra.

In this question, you are matching letters to numbers.

For example, if the numbers are 3 and 4, and the equation is **A − B = 1**, then you can work out that **A is 4** and **B is 3** because **4-3=1**. It wouldn't work the other way round because 3-4 does not equal 1!

In each part, match the numbers you have been given below to the capital letters to make the sums correct.

a) 1   5

$A + B = 6$

$A - B = 4$

b) 2   5
8   50

$A \div B = 10$

$B \times C = 10$

$C + D = 10$

c) 2   3
5   7

$A \times B \times C = 42$

$B + C + D = 10$

$D - B = 2$

d) 12   15
16   18
25   26
27   30

$A - B = 1$

$C \div D = 2$

$E + F = 30$

$G \times H = 400$

$F - G = 2$

8 Buruied treasure

Maths is used for all sorts of things: following map coordinates, spending money, even when competing in sports leagues.

A sailor is trying to leave us a clue about what they want for their birthday. They've sent us a copy of a map and their sailing log:

- I started the day where my boat is on the map. I took notes of my coordinates everywhere I stopped, beginning with my start location.

- I travelled 7 squares south and then 2 west, where I said hello to my penguin friend.

- The next part of my trip took me 5 squares east followed by 4 squares north. In spite of not having anywhere to land, I spent a while enjoying the view.

- My next stop involved travelling 3 squares east (to avoid bothering a sea monster) and then 5 squares north.

- Finally, I went as far west as my map would allow and then moved south until I was level with my starting position. This is where I ended my journey.

Using all of this information, can you work out what item of clothing is on the sailor's birthday list?

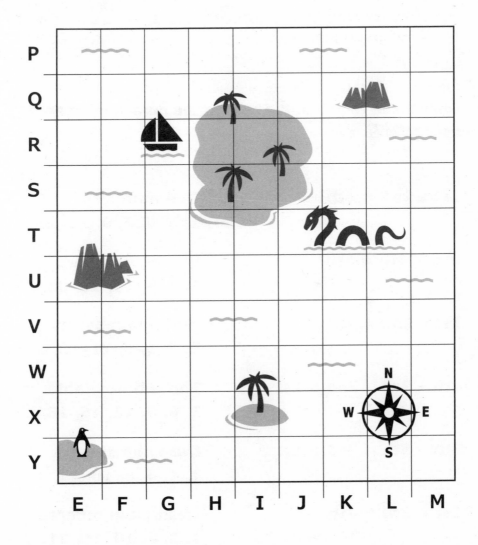

9 Mixed-up sums

The sums below appear to make no sense, but they can be made right!

For example, the first six prime numbers are: 2, 3, 5, 7, 11, 13, so the sum 1st + 3rd = 4th really means the sum 2 + 5 = 7.

Draw a line to match the sum to the number sequence used to create it.

1st x 2nd = 6th

3rd + 4th = 5th

1st x 2nd = 4th

4th − 3rd − 2nd = 1st

8th − 5th = 3rd + 1st

1st + 3rd = 4th

Odd numbers:
1, 3, 5, 7, 9, 11, ...

Square numbers:
1, 4, 9, 16, 25, 36, ...

Prime numbers:
2, 3, 5, 7, 11, 13, ...

Three times table:
3, 6, 9, 12, 15, 18, ...

Even numbers:
2, 4, 6, 8, 10, 12, ...

Triangle numbers:
1, 3, 6, 10, 15, 21, ...

10 The magic number

Playing around with numbers gives rise to many fun puzzles. For these ones, you have to think about whole numbers, e.g. 34, and the digits that form them, e.g. 3 and 4. The product of two numbers is what you get when you multiply them together – so the product of 3 and 4 is 12.

a) I'm thinking of a 2-digit number.
Both the digits are square numbers.
The whole number is a square number.
What is my number?

b) I'm thinking of another 2-digit number.
The digits are prime numbers. The whole number is the product of two prime numbers. All four of these prime numbers are different from each other.
What is my number?

c) I'm thinking of a 3-digit number, where none of the digits are zero. Removing the first digit gives a 2-digit square number. Removing the last digit also gives a 2-digit square number. Adding the digits together does not give a prime number
What is my number?

THE STORY OF GCHQ:
Sum of our parts

GCHQ has always been a world leader in mathematics. One incredible mathematician during the Second World War was Dr Max Newman. He was Alan Turing's teacher at Cambridge University and was recruited to work at Bletchley Park.

He was asked to set up a special team to investigate the new German Lorenz cypher machine. A mistake from a German operator, who was working the machine, meant that the Allies could understand how the machine created codes – three years before they saw a real live version!

The code was cracked, but Dr Newman realised they would need a new machine to do the decrypting as speedily as possible. He asked the Post Office (under the leadership of a brilliant engineer called Tommy Flowers) to build a machine, called COLOSSUS, which took them nine months. It was the world's first electronic computer and the origin of the modern computers that we use now.

More recently, the work of GCHQ mathematicians resulted in something that is still used to this day. In the early 1970s, James Ellis, Malcolm Williamson and Clifford Cocks helped create a new and complicated algorithm that protects us online when we are banking or shopping. It is called Public Key Cryptography and would remain a secret until 1997! Get ready to find out more about Public Key Cryptography in the coming pages.

The Lorenz cypher machine

11 Crossing in Königsberg

In the eighteenth century, Leonhard Euler invented Graph Theory, the study of how things are connected. He showed that it was impossible to walk around his town of Königsberg crossing each of the seven bridges only once, and without crossing the river in any other way.

In three of the plans below, it is possible to cross each bridge exactly once in a single walk.

Can you work out which is the actual plan of Königsberg, in which this is not possible?

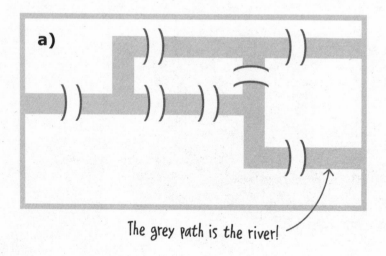

a)

The grey path is the river!

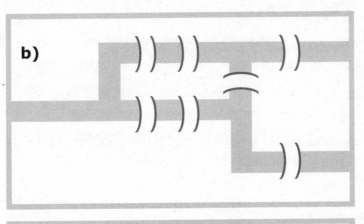

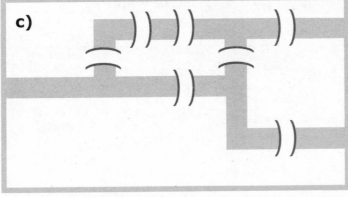

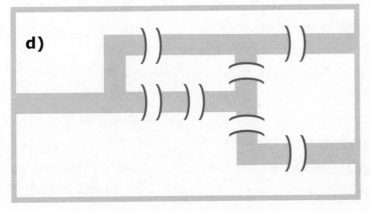

MADE IN GCHQ
Public Key Cryptography

You've probably seen the adults in your life buying something over the internet. They'll need to enter their bank details as they do their online shopping – but it's really important no one else can see these, because they might be able to steal money!

THE INTERNET

We need to arrange a secret key with the shop, so only they can see the bank details . . .

But we can't just send the secret key over the internet, as then everyone else will see it. So what else can we do? Well, in 1973, GCHQ mathematician genius Cliff Cocks – and his fellow workers – invented something called **Public Key Cryptography**, which magically solves this problem.

It's a bit like if the online shop sent us an unlocked padlock, but kept hold of the key. Anyone can see the padlock, but no one knows what key opens it.

We receive the unlocked padlock, and can use it to lock our bank details into a box. We then send the locked box back to the shop. Everyone saw the padlock, and everyone can see the locked box, but only the shop can open it!

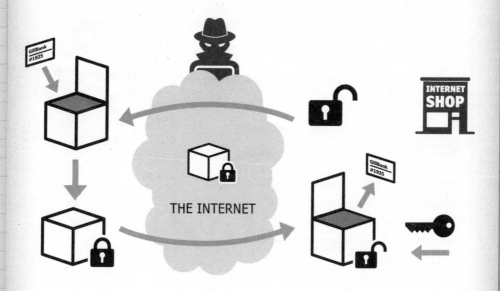

Sadly, we can't send real padlocks over the internet, but Cliff realised that we could send a **mathematical padlock** instead.

The shop picks two large numbers as its secret key. It then multiplies them together to give a huge number, and sends this to us. This huge number is the mathematical padlock, and is called the Public Key because everyone can see it, but no-one can work out which two numbers were multiplied together to produce it.

Cliff's method lets us use this Public Key to send a message over the internet, and then on to the shop, without anyone else seeing it. This is how we can buy things online without other people stealing our money!

Cliff's invention was kept secret, but it was re-invented in the outside world in 1978 by Ronald Rivest, Adi Shamir and Leonard Adleman. The algorithm became known as RSA, based on their initials and is now widely used online.

PEOPLE FROM OUR PAST

NAME:

Alan Turing

ROLE:

Codebreaker

FACT:

Alan Turing was a codebreaker extraordinaire who was in charge of the team that broke the Enigma code. Along with Dr Newman, his interest in mathematics led him to invent the early version of the computers that we use today.

DID YOU KNOW?

The face of the 2021 £50 note, Turing is an inspiration – a scientific genius who helped shorten the Second World War. He is one of the most iconic LGBTQ+ figures in the world, and embraced for his brilliance. Yet back in the 1950s he was treated terribly and branded a criminal, just because he was gay. These events led him to take his own life. His legacy reminds us of how hugely important it is to accept and celebrate everyone.

12 Padlock pairs

Using a calculator, find the pairs of secret numbers in the list on the left that you need to write on each key, so that they multiply together to unlock each padlock's **Public Key**:

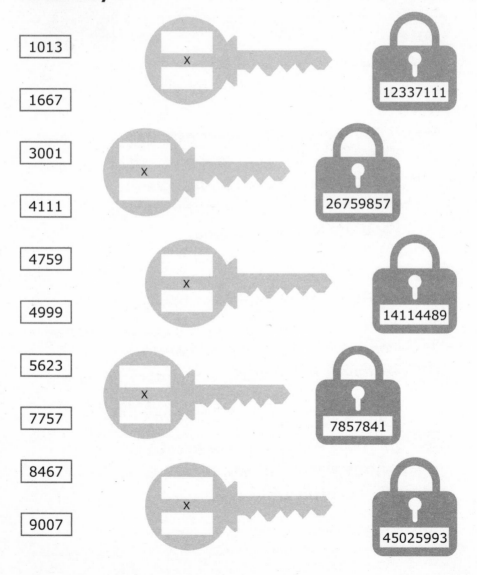

1013

1667

3001

4111

4759

4999

5623

7757

8467

9007

X 12337111

X 26759857

X 14114489

X 7857841

X 45025993

13 Crack the safe

To codebreak RSA, we would have to work out two secret numbers that can be multiplied together to give the Public Key number. It should be impossible to find them. However, if the secret numbers are not generated randomly enough then it might be possible.

Perhaps one of the secret numbers is small? Using a calculator, can you find two secret whole numbers, greater than 1, that multiply together to give the following RSA Public Keys?

a) 992102   b) 861395   c) 700021

....

14 Feeling confident?

Or perhaps the two secret numbers are almost equal to each other?

Can you find two secret whole numbers that multiply together to give the following RSA Public Keys?

a) 67765823   b) 64160099   c) 80999999

FUN FACTS

We have lots of groups at GCHQ that allow us to do fun stuff outside work. There are all sorts – from board gaming and gardening to running clubs and a choir.

Lots of mathematicians at GCHQ still prefer to use blackboards and chalk to do their sums and working out, so in some areas there's not a whiteboard in sight!

Pneumatic tubes used to run between offices in our old Oakley site. These are a network of tubes that can pass solid objects very quickly from room to room or building to building. They do this using compressed air! Nowadays we have emails and phones, of course, but back then the tubes were used to send documents, messages and the odd chocolate eclair! It was even used by a shy analyst to propose to his partner. She said yes (in person!).

Hints

1 The left-hand set of letters on each of the brick options will be the second half of a word, and the right-hand set will be the first half of the word. For the top line, you need to find the SECOND half of a word starting SEC.

2 Working along the top row from the 2 should be quite straightforward. Starting with 2, add 4 and divide by 3. That leaves you with 2 again in the third square along, so you just need to work out what number you add 1 to, to get 2. Other ones are more complicated, but you can work them out by a process of elimination. In the four squares in the bottom left, for instance, you know that the number you need to multiply by 3 has to be less than 4, as you can't have a number bigger than 9. So what number do you need to add 3 to, to get a number less than 4 (and remember you can use 0)?

3 To get you started, we'll tell you that there are: 12 inches in a foot, 3 feet in a yard and 1,760 yards in a mile. There are 1,000 millimetres in a metre and 1,000 metres in a kilometre. There are 25.4 millimetres in an inch.

4   For part **a)**, you just need to move a matchstick to change one single number. For parts **b)** to **d)**, you need to move a matchstick from one number to another. For parts **e)** and **f)**, maybe something more cunning is needed!

5   For parts **a)** and **b)**, think about each number in turn starting at 1 (or ONE), and carry on until you reach an answer. For part **c)**, note that you don't need to worry about numbers above 99, as they must all contain one of the words HUNDRED, THOUSAND, MILLION, etc., all of which have letters with enclosed spaces.

6   Try writing the numbers in the puzzle as words and see what you can spot!

7   For part **a)**, look at the second sum first. For part **b)**, look at the top sum first.

8   Draw out the route on the map, then look at the coordinates of each square where the sailor stopped!

9   Start with 1st × 2nd = 6th, as this is the most straightforward sum. For each sequence, multiply the first two numbers together. Does the answer equal the sixth number in the sequence? If so, then that one is solved and you can eliminate it when working out the other links.

10 Here are some handy tips for each question part:
    a) Only 0, 1, 4 and 9 are square numbers with one digit.

b) Only 2, 3, 5 and 7 are one-digit prime numbers.

c) The first two digits are a 2-digit square number, and these all end with one of 1, 4, 5, 6 or 9. This is the first digit of the last two digits, which is also a square, so what options exist for each possibility?

11 This problem puzzled the great mathematician Euler, so don't feel bad about looking at the hint! Count the number of bridge-ends that are on each of the four land areas. If you go over a bridge in the middle of your trip to get to one of the land areas, you need to leave via another bridge. That means you pass through two bridge-ends. When in your trip is this not the case?

12 Try each pair of numbers in turn. This isn't really a hint – it just shows you how difficult it can be to work out a puzzle like this, which is why a Public Key is so secure!

13 In each part, look for a small prime number that you can divide the code by to find a big whole number, which would form the second part of the code.

14 For each part, begin by taking the square root of the number. Maybe the two code numbers are close to this? (The square root of a number is another number which produces the first number when it is multiplied by itself. For example, 3x3 = 9. So 3 is the square root of 9.)

Chapter Seven

CODING

Speaking to computers

Hello! My name is Greg and I work in coding. Coding is the process of writing computer programs to enable a computer to perform a particular task. It's really important to GCHQ because it enables us to perform awesome jobs that a human could never do by themselves. I really enjoy watching my own programs being used – I get to see how I make a real impact.

When I was at school, I was really into science and PE. In fact, before I joined GCHQ I used to represent Team GB in sport and competed in the European Championships. (Our important work at GCHQ means keeping our identities secret and protecting our personal information, so I can't tell you which sport I'm afraid, as very clever puzzlers might be able to track me down!)

In my spare time, I love making my own codes and puzzles and sending them to my friends, to see if they can figure them out. Puzzling is great because it allows people to come together and work towards a common goal. Plus, it's just really fun when you get the right answer! My favourite type of puzzle is one

in which you need to break a code and find a secret message – so I'm looking forward to having a go at the codebreaking chapter in this book myself!

Since I began working at GCHQ, I've been taught every skill that I need to do my job. One great thing about the work I do is that you don't need to be a computer expert to do it – you just need to have a curious brain and be willing to learn.

As I have dyslexia and ADHD, I approach problems in different ways from lots of other people. At GCHQ, thinking differently helps me find solutions that others might not have seen.

The most challenging thing about my role is keeping track of time! It's easy for me to get so focused on the task I'm doing that the day flies by. Is there anything you enjoy doing so much that time just goes really quickly? I have all sorts of alarms and notes that tell me when I should be doing something, and they help me stay on track.

The computer programs we write are often very complicated, and we need to write them in a very precise way so the computer does exactly what we want. When we're done, we always check the programs to make sure the end result is what we were after. And if it's not, we have to change what we've written in the program until it does what we need it to!

All the puzzles in this chapter will test these skills, which are essential if you're going to be a good coder. A lot of this is trial and error – that is, trying out a particular instruction and seeing if you get the right result or not. If you don't, that's OK – it's all about trying again, so don't worry.

Good luck, puzzlers!

Greg

1 Missed connections

I've just been told that some visitors to GCHQ are lost! We need to find the visitors and get them to the places they're supposed to be.

We've been given some information about where they were last seen, and their method of travel.

I've also been given a map of the United Kingdom and Ireland. It has been marked with various locations, and the methods of travel are shown in lines across the map.

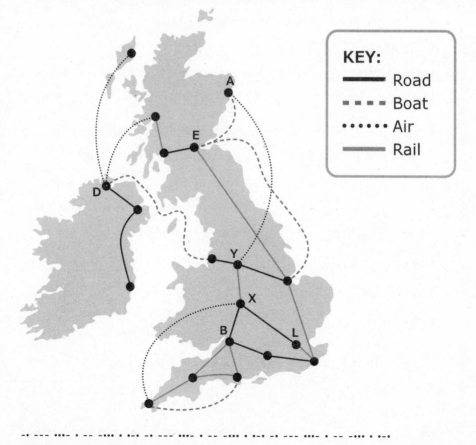

KEY:
- ▬▬▬ Road
- ▪ ▪ ▪ ▪ Boat
- • • • • • • Air
- ▬▬▬ Rail

Computer programs are sets of instructions, and as a programmer I need to be able to write and follow instructions precisely. See if you can use this skill to answer the following questions and help our lost visitors:

a) Starting from **L**, a group of visitors travelled by ROAD to **X** and then by RAIL to **Y**. Then they took an AIR route and a BOAT route and stopped. Where was their final destination?

b) Another group of visitors started at **L** and followed the same pattern of travel, but continued to repeat that pattern: ROAD–RAIL–AIR–BOAT (then back to ROAD and keep repeating). At which location would they get stuck and be unable to follow the instructions?

c) A third group started at **E** and wanted to see how many different places they could visit (with locations marked by letters) just by using RAIL and ROAD routes. How many could they visit (excluding their start location, **E**)?

d) One visitor refuses to travel by ROAD, but needs to get from **L** to **Y**. Can they?

e) An engineer needs to provide support to **E**, **L** and **D**. She can only live a maximum of 2 links away. Which location could she be based at?

FUN FACTS

Our work takes us around the world. We provide support to the UK Armed Forces and have done so in every campaign they have been involved in since the Second World War.

In fact, over 300 of our staff have been awarded medals for the work they have done in support of our Armed Forces.

Any fans of *Lord of the Rings*? Records in our archives show that JRR Tolkien expressed an interest in joining our codebreaking team during the 1930s.

-- --- ....- . -- -....- . .-.. -. .-. ---- ....- . -- -....- . .-.- -. .-. ---- ....- . -- -....- . .-.-

2 Vend-a-hand, please!

Coding allows you to create awesome devices and machines. I've thought up an idea for a vending machine that I monitor. You don't choose what snack you want from it – instead, you put your money in the coin tray, and it gives you something based on things like the time of day and what your name is!

Now that I have come up with my vending-machine idea, we need to test whether or not it will work. To do this, we need to use the information in the questions on the next page and a flow chart, to figure out who would get what. I also need these two important pieces of information:

- At the start of the week, the machine contains two bananas. No more bananas are loaded into the machine.

- Until the customer reaches a STOP, any money they have put into the machine is kept as credit.

A flow chart is like a kind of simple program, and in this puzzle we need to carefully check a set of instructions to find out a result – something we do a lot of in coding.

-· --- ····- · -- -···· · ·--· -· --- ····- · -- -···· · ·--· -· --- ····- · -- -···· · ·--

a) On Monday, Arthur (a coder) put £1 in at 4 p.m. What would have come out?

b) On Tuesday, Isobel (a non-coder) put £2 in at 1 p.m. What would have come out?

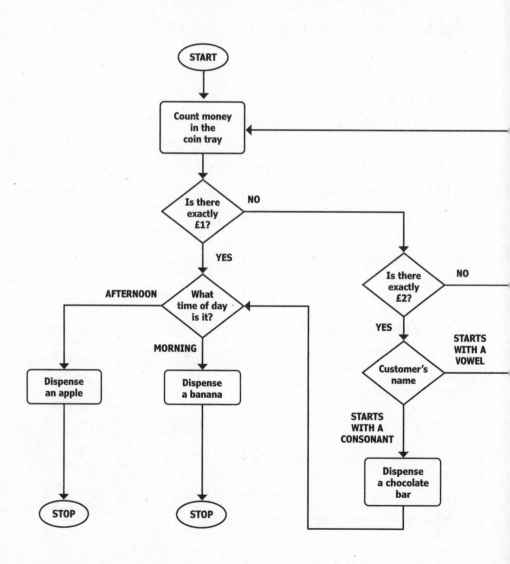

c) On Wednesday, Jack (a non-coder) put £1 in at 10.30 a.m. What would have come out?

d) On Thursday, Khalid (a coder) put £3 in at 3 p.m. What two products would have come out?

e) On Friday, Khalid (still a coder!) goes back at 3 p.m. and puts another £3 in the machine. What does he get out this time? (Reminder: the machine has not been restocked all week.)

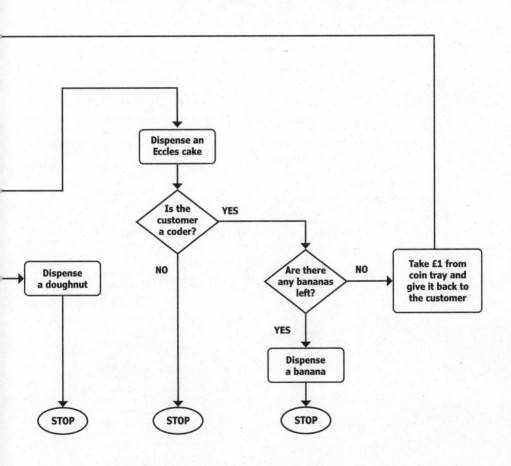

3 Difficult dataflow

We've practised doing instructions in order, but what happens when we don't have a strict order? This is called **dataflow**.

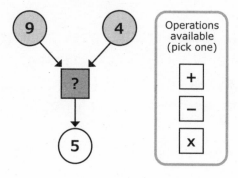

a) What operation do we need here to take the 9 and 4 and produce 5?

b) This next one is a bit trickier! Sometimes in coding we need to flow instructions into each other. See if you can figure out where each operation goes into this dataflow to result in 12.

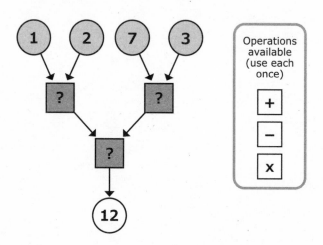

c) This one is even trickier. Now there are numbers to fill in as well as operations.

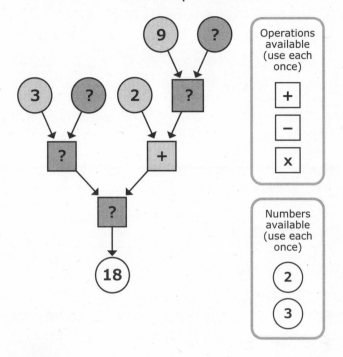

Operations available (use each once)

+

−

×

Numbers available (use each once)

2

3

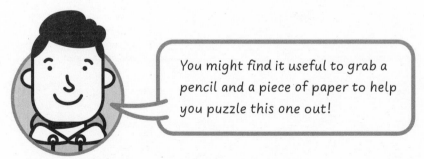

You might find it useful to grab a pencil and a piece of paper to help you puzzle this one out!

4 Fun functions

Sometimes we need to move whole chunks of instructions. We call these **functions**.

We have three functions below (**A**, **B** and **C**). What order do we need to put them in so they will combine to turn a 4 into an 8?

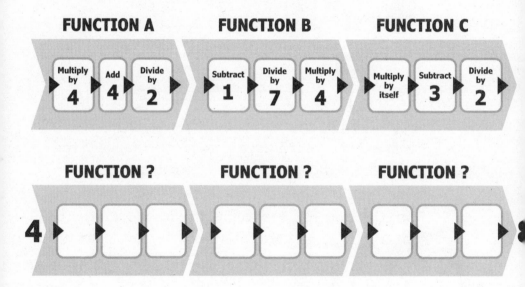

FUNCTION A

Multiply by **4** ▶ Add **4** ▶ Divide by **2**

FUNCTION B

Subtract **1** ▶ Divide by **7** ▶ Multiply by **4**

FUNCTION C

Multiply by itself ▶ Subtract **3** ▶ Divide by **2**

FUNCTION ?

FUNCTION ?

FUNCTION ?

4 ▶ □ ▶ □ ▶ □ ▶ □ ▶ □ ▶ □ ▶ □ ▶ □ ▶ □ ▶ 8

5 Dog days

Sometimes in coding we need to control multiple processes (or threads) at once so we can understand how they might interact.

Here's a good example. I've come across some people training their dogs in the park, and they need help controlling multiple dogs at once!

- In the diagram on the next page, there are three dogs: 1, 2 and 3.

- We also have ten platforms labelled from A to J.

- The shapes in the diagram allow us to direct the dogs to different platforms. If we shout one of the shapes attached to the platform that a dog is on, the dog will the follow the line leading from that shape to the platform the line is linked to.

For example, if we shouted 'square', dog 1 would go to platform E, dog 2 would go to platform D, and dog 3 would go to platform G.

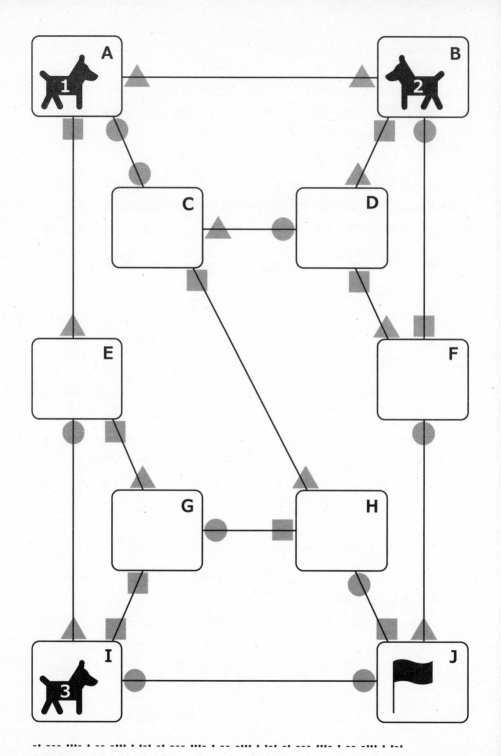

RULES:

1. All dogs will follow all commands. You cannot give individual commands to individual dogs.
2. You are allowed to have more than one dog per platform.
3. Dogs on platform J will not 'stay' there, but will keep moving until all three are there at the same time.

Now see if you can answer the following questions:

a) Suppose the only dog was dog 1 on platform A. Can you provide a series of five commands to get it to visit platforms B and I, and finish at platform J, without shouting 'square'?

for these next three questions you can use more than five commands.

b) Could you do the same route as in question **a)**, but with 'triangle' as the forbidden command? If yes, state the commands; if not, explain why.

c) Could you do the same tour as in question **a)**, but now with 'circle' as the forbidden command? If yes, state the commands; if not, explain why.

d) Suppose all three dogs are now starting in the positions as shown in the diagram. What series of commands can you shout to get them to all finish at platform J at the same time?

THE STORY OF GCHQ:
Keeping secrets

The use of codes to keep messages secret is not new. In 1586, a plot to assassinate Queen Elizabeth I was hatched using secret messages sent by letter. Queen Elizabeth I had a spymaster called Sir Francis Walsingham who managed to break the code used by the plotters and disrupt the plan.

As you probably know by now, Bletchley Park was our Second World War home and was a very secret place. People would travel there not knowing what they were going to be doing and often not being able to tell anyone where they were off to. It was home to huge teams of codebreakers whose work led to the building of the world's first computer, called the COLOSSUS.

-. --- .... . . -- .... . .-. .- .--- .... . . -.. .... . .-. .- .- .--- .... . .-.

The COLOSSUS (pictured) was just that, a colossus! Occupying a space the size of a living room and weighing five tonnes, it was built to crack the codes of a very complicated code machine used by the German military, called the Lorenz. This was even used by the Nazi leader, Adolf Hitler. A very famous codebreaker called Bill Tutte (who you met in the Engineering chapter) managed to work out the code by using just a piece of paper and a pencil.

The COLOSSUS computer

6 Have you got what it takes?

In coding, we have to do a lot of sorting to get the right results.

For this puzzle, we've got lots of new candidates coming for an interview at GCHQ (like you might do one day!) and they need to get to the right rooms.

To direct them, we need to make sure we're putting the correct sign at each junction in the main interview hall.

Opposite is the map of the main hall. You can see there are three staircases – 1, 2 and 3 – where candidates will enter, and they'll always travel in the direction of the arrow.

Then they'll get to the junctions – A, B, C or D – where they'll read the sign. If the answer to the sign is 'yes', they'll go left; if it's 'no', they'll go right, as shown on the map. Only one sign is allowed per junction.

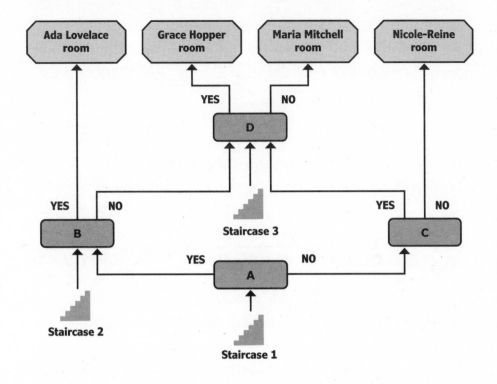

Each candidate has a different code number:

NAME	CODE NUMBER
Alice	9451
Bob	6311
Charlie	3486
Dani	7196

NAME	CODE NUMBER
Ed	8878
Fred	4562
George	2369
Harry	7452

Here are the signs you need to place. Each one has a question that can be answered yes or no, and it refers to the candidate's code numbers listed on page 217.

1. IS YOUR CODE NUMBER MORE THAN 5,000?

2. IS YOUR CODE NUMBER EVEN?

3. IS THE FIRST DIGIT OF YOUR CODE NUMBER EVEN?

4. IS THE LAST DIGIT OF YOUR CODE NUMBER MORE THAN 5?

Can you answer the following questions, and help direct candidates to the correct rooms?

a) Alice and Bob are attending an interview but cannot be in the same room. They will walk up Staircase 3, so which out of Sign 1 or Sign 3 should we put at Junction D to separate them?

b) The next day, Charlie, Dani and Ed are attending an interview and cannot be in the same room as each other. They will arrive via Staircase 2. Which out of Sign 1 or Sign 3 should we put at Junction B, and which at Junction D?

c) The next day, Bob, Charlie, Dani and Ed are all now arriving via Staircase 3. They need to be split up so we end up with two people in two separate interview rooms. Which sign out of the set of four should we use?

d) The following week, all attendees will be arriving via Staircase 1. We must put Sign 2 up at Junction A. At which junctions do we put the other three signs so that the rooms have the following attendees:

Ada Lovelace: Ed & Fred
Grace Hopper: Dani & Harry
Maria Mitchell: Charlie & George
Nicole-Reine: Alice & Bob

e) The week after, all attendees will be arriving again via Staircase 1. This time, we must put Sign 4 at Junction C. What signs do we put at Junctions A, B and D to split people into the following rooms:

Ada Lovelace: Bob & Ed
Grace Hopper: Charlie, Dani & Fred
Maria Mitchell: George
(on their own doing an exam)
Nicole-Reine: Alice & Harry

7 It's in the net

In programming, a **string** is a set of characters, which could be letters, numbers or symbols.

At GCHQ, we often have to process strings to enable us to do our jobs.

a) Let's have a look at some basic string processing. I want the output to be TENNIS, but I'm only getting TENIS. Can you spot where this is going wrong and find the easiest way to fix it?

NETBALL → Remove 'ball' → NET → Reverse letters → TEN → Add 'IS' → TENIS

b) Can you match the available actions 1 to 4 to their locations A to D in the flow below?

LONG JUMP → A → LONG → B → LOG → C → GOL → D → GOLF

ACTIONS AVAILABLE:

1) Reverse characters

2) Remove last 4 characters

3) Add 'F'

4) Remove 3rd character

c) Can you match the available actions 1 to 3 with the locations A to C in the flow below, and fill in the missing words? (They don't need to be proper words!)

| CRICKET | A | ? | B | ? | C | HOCKEY |

ACTIONS AVAILABLE:

1) Replace 6th letter with 'Y'

2) Replace 'CR' with 'H'

3) Replace 3rd character with 'O'

PEOPLE FROM OUR PAST

NAME:
Charlotte 'Betty' Webb

ROLE:
Codebreaker

FACT:
She once described how, at just eighteen, she joined the top secret mission at Bletchley Park to 'do something more for the war effort than just bake sausage rolls'!

DID YOU KNOW?
Charlotte Webb grew up with a German nanny, which meant she learned German. It was this knowledge of the language that helped her to decrypt top secret German radio messages during the Second World War.

8 Tommy's Flowers

Sometimes when coding, we need to be able to allocate resources (like memory, processing and disk space) in a clever way so that they meet certain rules. This skill may be useful for this next puzzle.

My friend Tommy is trying to win the GCHQ flower show. He has three roses, three tulips and two dahlias. He must present all eight flowers on the table in a straight line.

According to the rules of the GCHQ flower show, they need to be arranged so that:

- Each of the three roses has exactly one flower between it and the next rose.
- Each of the tulips has at least two flowers between it and the next tulip.
- One dahlia is immediately to the right of a rose.
- One dahlia is immediately to the right of a tulip.

How might Tommy arrange the flowers?

9 You only move twice

As a programmer, you need to know how to put instructions together to get amazing results.

At GCHQ we play a board game used to train all our super spies – the full rules are very complex and TOP SECRET. Last year we had a competition, and I reached the final!

Opposite is how the board looked during the semi-final. The person on E2 shows my character's position, and I had the following two cards in my hand:

a) Can you say how I used my two cards to get on to the escape helicopter on A3 to win the game?

b) After I won that game, I got to the final. Amazingly, in that match we reached exactly the same board positions again! Except this time I had to escape via the seaplane (on E7) and I had the following two additional cards (so four in total):

CARD 3
MOVE A
SATELLITE DISH
ONE HEX

CARD 4
ADD **ONE** TO ANY
NUMBERS CONTAINED
IN THE NEXT
CARD PLAYED

Can you say how I used the four cards to get
onto the seaplane hex and win the finals?

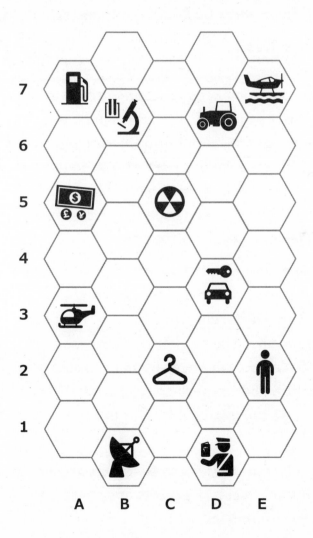

Hints

1 For part **b)**, you already know the route the visitors are taking. You now need to work out where they could go to by ROAD from the final destination in part **a)**, and then where they can go from there by RAIL. And then keep going!

2 The trick with this question is to follow the instructions precisely. For each question, start at the top and follow the arrows. Make sure you keep following arrows until you reach a box that says STOP. For later parts, the number of bananas and the amount of money in the coin tray are important, especially in part **e)**. You could try keeping track of them on a piece of paper. Remember that if the machine gives money back to the customer, the amount in the coin tray will be different!

3 For part **a)**, you need to pick the operation that, when applied to 9 and 4, gets you to 5. For part **b)**, try working it out using the three different sums for that final box in turn. The operation in the top box in each case can't be in the lower boxes, so you have already reduced your options! For part **c)**, don't expect an easy answer! Try rewriting it as three separate puzzles, as in the hint for part **b)**.

4 Just because all the numbers in the functions are whole numbers, that doesn't mean the result of a function needs to be a whole number!

-·· --- ····- · -- -···· · ·-· -· --- ····- · -- -···· · ·-· -· --- ····- · -- -···· · ·-·

5 For question **a)**, the dog has to finish at J, but that doesn't mean it can't visit J before it finishes there! For questions **b)** and **c)**, if you can't seem to solve these, then analyse why you keep failing. What is causing the failure? Is it always effectively the same reason? For question **d)**, if you find this tricky (as it is!), try starting with just two dogs, and get them on to the same platform. Once on the same platform, they are effectively only one dog!

6 For each part, you have to imagine the candidates approaching the sign and working out which way they should go. Each of them would look at their code number to see what the sign means for them, based on whether it is above 5000, is even, has an even first digit, or has a last digit above 5. You could work this out for all of the candidates and write the answers down. That will help you to work out which sign divides the candidates as needed.

7 For question **a)**, look at each instruction. Could one be changed only slightly to get to TENNIS? For question **b)**, try each operation in turn. Which is the first one? That will reduce your options for the others. For question **c)**, the word HOCKEY has six letters. Does this give a clue to which instruction is C?

8 Try writing out how the roses must be spaced from each other. Do the same with the tulips. How can both of these be achieved with only eight spaces?

9 For both parts, the position of the satellite dish is the most important thing!

Chapter Eight
CYBER SECURITY

Staying safe online

Hello! My name is Sandeep and I'm a cyber security researcher based at GCHQ's Manchester office.

I work at a part of GCHQ called the National Cyber Security Centre (NCSC). We help keep people and organisations in the UK safe online by giving everyone tools and advice on how to improve their online security. One piece of advice is to have a strong and separate password for your email – you'll find this a useful tip for one of the questions in this chapter!

A cyber attack could involve people accessing your online accounts or computer systems that they shouldn't have access to (this is often called **hacking**). An attack could also try to make computer systems do things they shouldn't or give access to your personal information which can cause harm to you or an organisation.

Cyber security was actually a bit of a hobby of mine before I decided to apply for a job at GCHQ. I happened to watch a video on YouTube explaining what cyber security meant and how cyber security

workers use their skills and knowledge to protect people and organisations from attackers. I found this really interesting, so I started a course that would teach me the basics. I knew I wanted to do my part to help protect the UK from cyber attacks, which are one of the biggest threats we face as a country, so GCHQ was the ideal choice.

The NCSC works on something called defensive cyber. Defensive cyber involves protecting organisations and people from cyber attacks, while cyber operations (something people at NCSC also work on) make sure that the people doing these attacks aren't able to operate online.

Perhaps you've played football or netball? Think of cyber operations as the people trying to score the goals for your team, while defensive cyber are the people trying to protect your goal so that your opponent doesn't score. Our opponents could be fraudsters, criminals or even other countries. While our opponents don't always play by the rules, GCHQ does, which means we always work within the law.

In my job as a cyber security researcher, I spend a

lot of time looking at how we can improve the security of technology used by people and organisations, to help prevent cyber attacks. This involves a lot of testing and experimenting with different types of technology. We simulate cyber attacks, which means we pretend to attack certain pieces of technology, so we can spot weaknesses – places where attacks might be able to get through – and then work to make that technology stronger.

Before coming to GCHQ, I had a job as a social worker where I helped adults with learning difficulties in my community. I really liked that job, as I felt I was making positive changes, but I wanted to combine helping people with my love for technology. GCHQ has been the perfect place to find all of this.

In my spare time I like to keep fit at the gym. I also enjoy listening to audiobooks. If I can, I like doing spot-the-difference puzzles or wordsearches too. Puzzling helps me in my work, as I have to problem-solve all the time, think creatively and find patterns. You may find these skills useful in this chapter of cyber puzzles.

Good luck!   Sandeep

1 Word decoder

This first question is the perfect introduction to cyber security – or at least it would be if some hackers hadn't messed with the file!

I need your help to unscramble the words and phrases below, which all relate to cyber security in some way.

The numbers **[1]** to **[9]** show where the words or phrases should go.

[1] BATTLES (7)

[2] BY CITY RESCUER (5,8)

[3] COMET SPUR (9)

[4] INTRO SINUS (10)

[5] MAP SHORTENS (11)

[6] SETBACK TRACY (5,7)

[7] TAB ANY CIRCUITRY ELECTRON SEEN (8,5,8,6)

[8] TAPS LOP (7)

[9] TEN TRINE (8)

The numbers in brackets at the end show the length of the words.

One of the functions of cyber security is to protect the devices we all use (**[5]**, **[8]**, **[1]** and **[3]**), and the online services we access – both at home and at work – from **[6]**.

[2] is important because all these – and the **[9]** – are now such a part of our world that it's difficult to imagine how we'd manage to live without them.

Set up in 2016, the **[7]** (NCSC) is a part of GCHQ and is the UK's leading authority on cyber security, helping to make the UK the safest place to live and do business online.

The NCSC helps defend against national cyber attacks and provides advice to victims of cyber **[4]**.

2 Logging on

In order to help me with some cyber security, we need to get you logged on to your shiny new computer! A message has popped up asking you to create a new password.

A good password is one that isn't easy to guess, and not commonly used. We advise you to choose ThreeRandomWords – so not ComputerCyberPuzzles for example!

Which of these passwords should you use?

a) Springsummerautumnwinter

b) Password123

c) RainBallMango

3 A safe password

Now you've created a safe password for yourself, let's look at why other passwords are not so safe.

Hackers can use lots of different ways to access stuff that's private, so having strong, separate passwords and storing them safely is a good way to protect yourself online. But what does a strong password look like?

Many people swap out letters for numbers or special characters to try and make their password harder to work out, but this doesn't always make it a good password, as they can be easily guessed!

Can you guess the original word from these passwords?

a) **Pa55w0rd**

b) **L!V3RPOOL**

c) **$3Cur1TY**

d) **5P1D3rm4N**

e) **d!5N£yl@nD**

THE STORY OF GCHQ:
A voyage into cyberspace

At GCHQ, we love technology – and we want the UK to benefit from every advantage the digital age offers.

Almost everyone in the UK spends large parts of their daily life online; as well as using the internet for shopping and banking, millions socialise online daily – updating their social-media profile or making a video call to somebody on the other side of the country (or even on the other side of the world!).

But you need to use the internet safely and securely because criminals could be trying to steal your personal details – or even access your bank account. That's why we all need to practise basic cyber security to protect all of the internet-connected devices we use.

--- --- .-.. ..-. --- --- .-.. ..-. --- --- .-.. ..-. --- --- .-.. ..-.

Nowadays that's not just phones or computers, it means things like TVs, cars and even some fridges! Vast amounts of personal information are stored on our connected devices that need to be protected.

The National Cyber Security Centre (NCSC), which is part of GCHQ, was created in 2016. It is responsible for helping everyone in the UK to be as safe as possible online. Because you don't need to be an expert to put basic cyber security in place that will make your devices much safer.

For example, the most used (and so least safe) passwords are based on world famous football teams and music artists! It's much harder to guess a password made up of three random words than the names of one Premier League team, or this year's most streamed singer. You will explore more about the right ways to set up super secure passwords in this chapter.

4 Guess the password

We never want to forget our passwords, so people may use memorable information – such as pet names or favourite football teams – to create them. If hackers can get this information, they may be able to guess the password!

Using the social-media posts below, can you work out which password is being used?

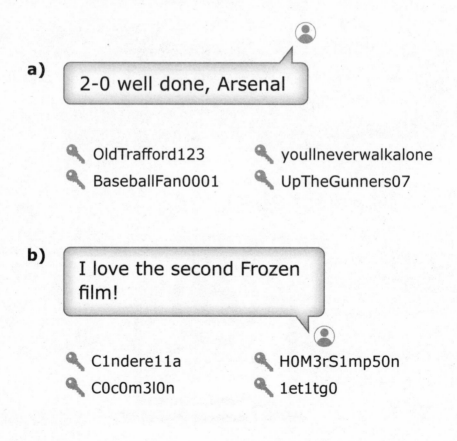

a)

2-0 well done, Arsenal

🔑 OldTrafford123   🔑 youllneverwalkalone
🔑 BaseballFan0001   🔑 UpTheGunners07

b)

I love the second Frozen film!

🔑 C1ndere11a   🔑 H0M3rS1mp50n
🔑 C0c0m3l0n   🔑 1et1tg0

c)

SO excited to get that trick right at the ramps today!

🔑 Sk8rGirl   🔑 B@ll3tLove
🔑 TennisStar   🔑 Lacr0sse

d)

#ThrowbackThursday – when my Luna met her new friend at the park

🔑 Labrador1010   🔑 ilovemyhamster
🔑 passwordmeow   🔑 qwerty98765

5 Safety is key

Sometimes, even after logging on successfully, we still need to prove who we are. This keeps devices extra safe from hackers.

To do this, there is a process called either two-step verification (2SV for short), or two-factor authentication (2FA). A code might be texted to us, or sent to an email address, that we then need to enter in order to access our device. We might also receive a code through an app (called an **authentication app**), or there might be an option for us to use a fingerprint scanner or a device that recognizes our face.

It prevents hackers from getting into your device even if they know or guess your password.

To find out which method of 2SV is best for me, I'd like to know which methods my fellow workers use on their devices. But I only have a few bits of information in order to work this out.

Using the following clues, can you complete the table below?

Clue 1: Beth uses the authentication app.

Clue 2: Neither Beth nor Mina have the phone.

Clue 3: The authentication app is on the laptop.

Clue 4: Whoever has the phone uses text messaging to authenticate.

		WHO			DEVICE		
		AMY	BETH	MINA	PHONE	TABLET	LAPTOP
METHHOD	TEXT MESSAGING		✗				
	FINGERPRINT READER		✗				
	AUTHENTICATION APP	✗	✓	✗			
DEVICE	PHONE						
	TABLET						
	LAPTOP						

6 Backing up

Not only do we need to keep the data on our devices safe, we also need to back it up. This means making a copy of it in case something happens to the original.

It's useful to know what types of data you might want to back up. Hidden in the grid opposite are six types of data – see if you can find them all. Each type of data follows directly on from the end of the previous one. The first two have been highlighted for you.

O	F	E	M	A	C	O	U
R	S	C	L	I	E	T	H
E	R	I	V	E	D	T	E
O	E	D	I	R	E	N	I
S	P	S	A	E	F	F	I
H	H	O	N	T	O	A	D
I	D	T	O	S	H	D	E
R	O	W	E	M	O	N	M
K	E	S	U	L	S	A	G
M	E	S	S	A	V	U	E
W	T	H	A	T	Y	O	I
L	S	G	G	E	L	S	O
H	I	N	M	S	M	E	O
T	Y	P	O	S	U	N	E
N	O	T	C	I	I	C	E

Let's back up a minute – literally! Trace a path back up from the letter where you ended to get back-up advice. You can reuse letters as you go.

7 New starters

> A place on a computer where individual information – such as a username and password – is stored, so a person can access personal information, or data held by an organisation.

We need to set up profiles on computers for four people at a hospital: **River, Zahra, Zeke and Lou.**

The profile will need to be set up depending on what role each person has: **doctor, receptionist, paramedic and patient.**

The hospital holds personal and medical information on its patients. In order to keep this data secure, we need to set up **permissions**. Permissions make sure that people can only access and change the information they need. Permissions help keep confidential information safe.

The four permission types are:

CREATE and EDIT PERSONAL records ONLY

VIEW MEDICAL records ONLY

VIEW PERSONAL and MEDICAL records ONLY

VIEW and EDIT MEDICAL records ONLY

No two people have the same permissions.

Can you use the clues to help me work out what permissions each person has? To make it even harder, we don't yet know which person is in which role.

1 The receptionist needs to be able to register new patients, book appointments, and make sure that the patients' contact details are up to date. They will need permissions to CREATE and EDIT PERSONAL records ONLY.

2 The patient cannot EDIT any MEDICAL records.

3 Neither Zeke nor Lou have permission to EDIT MEDICAL records.

4 The paramedic needs to be able to VIEW a patient's MEDICAL records ONLY.

5 The paramedic's name starts with the letter Z.

6 Zahra should be able to VIEW MEDICAL records ONLY.

7 Zeke is not a patient.

	PATIENT	DOCTOR	RECEPTIONIST	PARAMEDIC	CREATE and EDIT PERSONAL records only	VIEW MEDICAL records ONLY	VIEW PERSONAL and MEDICAL records ONLY	VIEW and EDIT MEDICAL records ONLY
River								
Zahra								
Zeke								
Lou								
CREATE and EDIT PERSONAL records ONLY								
VIEW MEDICAL records ONLY								
VIEW PERSONAL and MEDICAL records ONLY								
VIEW and EDIT MEDICAL records ONLY								

As with previous questions, you might find this grid helpful!

NAME	ROLE	PERMISSIONS
River		
Zahra		
Zeke		
Lou		

FUN FACTS

In 2021, our National Cyber Security Centre disrupted over two million hacking attempts.

If you're on any GCHQ site, it's top secret, and that means no mobile phones so no selfies or photos!

Recycling and protecting the environment are important to us. When we shred top secret documents, the shreddings are used to create fertiliser, which then gets used to grow potatoes. Maybe your next bag of crisps could come from top secret potatoes!

--- --- .-.. ..-. --. --- .-.. ..-. --. --- .-.. ..-. --. --- .-.. ..-.

8 Phish and chips

Phishing is when attackers attempt to trick people into doing the wrong thing. This might be clicking a bad link that will download something harmful to their computer (**malware**), or tricking people into entering important personal information, such as bank details.

Phishing can be done by using text messages, social media, phone calls or email or by clicking on an advert. There may be things about the message that make you rightly suspicious!

a) Charlie has a bank account at Gloucester Bank. One day the following email arrived:

To: Charlie43233@coldmail.com
From: kim@glocesterbank.com

Hello Charlie,

This is Kim from Gloucester Bank. The attached file provides information relevant to your account. It is important that you read this.

Kim

What might make Charlie suspicious about this email? After all, they get lots of emails from Gloucester Bank with important information.

b) Charlie bought their mobile phone from Phone Company. The following email arrived:

To: Charlie43233@coldmail.com
From: Chris@phonecompany.com

Hello Charlie,

Our technical team have discovered a problem with your phone. We can fix this remotely. Please send us your password by return so that we can do this.

Thank you,
Chris
Customer Relationship Manager
Phone Company

What might make Charlie suspicious about this email?

c) The following day this email arrived:

To: Charlie43233@coldmail.com
From: Chris@phonecompany.com

Hello Charlie,

You didn't respond to my previous email. I
understand that – I expect you didn't want to
send your password in an email. Very sensible.
However, the problem with your phone is that
the security is not up to date, and we believe
criminals will be accessing your phone in the
next 24 hours. So please ring this number to
give me your password: 01045 307475.

Thank you,
Chris
Customer Relationship Manager
Phone Company

Why might Charlie also find this email suspicious?

d) Charlie is a fan of the band Thunder, and is on the fan club mailing list. One day this email arrived:

To: Charlie43233@coldmail.com

From: lightning@thunderband.com

Hello

A special offer for Thunder fans!

Tickets for an extra concert on the next tour!

Get your name on the list early – first 50 people to reply will get tickets for just £1! That's right – £1!!

Click on this link IMMEDIATELY so you don't miss out!

Why might Charlie be suspicious of this email?

9 Cyber search

Introducing . . .
the National Cyber Force

Being active online is an important part of everyday life – from streaming sites to online gaming, doing our shopping to scrolling social media. Unfortunately, these same online spaces (and more) are also used by those who want to do us harm:

- Cybercriminals want to use the internet to steal money.

- They may also want to damage our devices through viruses and ransomware (i.e. demanding money).

- Harmful organisations may want to spread fake news designed to cause division.

The National Cyber Force (NCF) uses amazing cutting-edge technology, and works with other countries around the world to protect against threats in cyberspace. We work behind the scenes using cyber as a tool to stop people with bad intentions from achieving their goals.

We are made up of people from the UK's intelligence agencies (GCHQ and MI6), and from the Ministry of Defence, DSTL and the Armed Forces – civilian and military – all working together to make the country a safer place.

Find words from the text on the previous page in this wordsearch.

To help, here are the lengths of the words you need to find:

- One 10-letter word
- One 9-letter word
- Three 8-letter words
- Two 7-letter words
- Three 6-letter words
- Five 5-letter words
- One two-word phrase (8 letters)

Y	E	N	O	M	F	O	R	C	E
S	G	A	M	I	N	G	P	N	I
W	S	O	I	M	E	D	I	A	M
E	T	A	L	R	T	L	N	R	P
N	A	T	I	O	N	A	L	M	O
E	E	E	T	O	N	R	A	E	R
K	R	S	A	H	I	H	I	D	T
A	H	P	R	O	T	E	C	T	A
F	T	C	Y	B	E	R	O	E	N
G	N	I	P	P	O	H	S	P	T

The unused letters in the grid will spell out a word that describes what the National Cyber Force is. What is this word?

PEOPLE FROM OUR PAST

NAME:

Pamela Pigeon

ROLE:

Station Commander

FACT:

Pamela was the first female Station Commander to take charge of an interception site – a place that worked on gathering information sent by the enemy during the Second World War. She was based at RAF Marston Montgomery on the edge of the Peak District, which was a group of wooden huts (and about a hundred people), and very isolated. She was only twenty-five years old when she joined up.

DID YOU KNOW?

Pamela took her role so seriously, she never revealed the work that she did. That's a long time to keep a secret!

Hints

1 **[5]**, **[8]**, **[1]** and **[3]** are all plural. They are also all different devices that you can use.

2 Remember that your password should be three random words.

3 Some special characters and numbers look like letters, so have been used to replace them. 0 looks like O, 1 and ! look like I, 5 looks like S.

4 **a)** Which football team is mentioned? What is their nickname?

b) Which film is mentioned? What do you know about it?

c) What sport involves ramps?

d) What sort of animal do you think Luna is?

5 Look at clue 2. Who has the phone? Put a tick in the appropriate box in the grid, and then you can add some crosses. Look at clue 3. Can you work out who is using the laptop now?

6 You only go down the grid and across to find the types of data. After **EMAIL** and **VIDEOS** comes **PHOTOS**. Then something particularly relevant to school!

For the return journey, you only go up and across.

7 Putting ticks and crosses in the grid for information you already know will really help you here. Try to work out who can **VIEW and EDIT MEDICAL records ONLY**. And then which job can **VIEW PERSONAL and MEDICAL records ONLY**.

8 **a)** Look carefully. Why might the email NOT actually be from Gloucester Bank?

b) Is Charlie being asked to do anything unsafe?

c) How do you think the email makes Charlie feel?

d) Is this a good offer?

9 Look at the text to see what words of each length might be in the grid.

When it comes to being secure online, our **top hints** are:

1 Use three random words to create harder to guess passwords: **CardiganSnailMOon!** is better than **Password123.**

2 2-Step Verification is a way of 'double checking' that a person is really who they say they are when logging into an online account.

3 If your device is asking you to install the latest update, do it as soon as possible! It's one of the most important things you can do to keep yourself safe online.

Team Challenge!

The final part of this book is the Team Challenge. This consists of seven puzzles, each themed around the individual chapters, together with a final puzzle which links the answers from these seven puzzles together.

Each of the seven puzzles has a single, short, answer, and you need to keep track of these. The table at the end of this section may help with this. Not all the answers are actual words, and some are numbers (and we had to make up the name of the bank!). You could have a go at this with your friends – and it will hopefully show the value of teamwork. We're afraid there are no hints or answers in the book for this challenge!

Three of the puzzles - and the final fiendish challenge - can be found in the colour section in the middle of the book

Colin

The suspects from the Analysis chapter are up to no good.

They have created a virus which has infected millions of computers around the world and it's set to DELETE THE INTERNET unless we can find and access the laptop, and enter a special STOP CODE to prevent it happening.

Unfortunately we don't know the STOP CODE, and the laptop is hidden in an unknown vault in an unknown bank in an unknown city. The laptop has a password we don't know, and is in an unknown deposit box with an unknown access code, accessible only by a robot that's been sabotaged.

Fortunately, we've got hold of some crucial information that will help us get what we need.

So grab your friends, along with a pen and paper, and see if you can save the internet!

CODEBREAKING

Meg

We've discovered three messages sent between our suspects. The first is from the group leader. We hope they contain useful information – but can you decrypt them to find out?

To: LAA

From: R8FPGLA

46 L8Z87P 5I55 LP 6S2U

KF LQF QFLCH PB VBMF LYFLC K0PY PYF TAL9. PY07 VF77LZF X87P QFMFLA7 PYF 9LVF BE PYF OL9W KYFQF PYF CFTB70P OBJ 07 ABDLPFC. E8QPYFQ 09EBQVLP0B9 K0AA EBAABK 7FTLQLPFAH.

To: R8FPGLA

From: QBO09

6 7FTPFVOFQ 5I55 LP I13N

HB8 C0C 9BP Z0MF PYF 9LVF BE PYF OL9W 09 HB8Q VF77LZF.

To: QBO09

From: R8FPGLA

6 7FTPFVOFQ 5I55 LP I12S

HB8 K0AA X87P YLMF PB ABBW YLQCFQ. PYF E0Q7P 2 AFPPFQ7 LQF L 9LVF. PYF AL7P 2 AFPPFQ7 LQF L 9LVF. EL0A09Z PYLP L7W OBO KY0PF

CODING

Greg

We have intercepted a flow chart that tells the robot how to find the deposit box once inside the vault.

You are looking for three numbers, which will program the robot correctly, so it can find the box.

The correct number entered into the START box will get you to the padlock at the end of the flow chart. But you must follow certain rules:

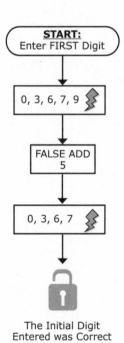

START:
Enter FIRST Digit

↓

0, 3, 6, 7, 9 ⚡

↓

FALSE ADD 5

↓

0, 3, 6, 7 ⚡

↓

The Initial Digit
Entered was Correct

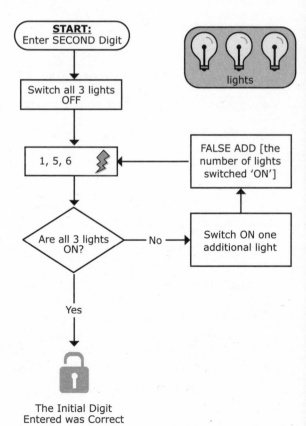

START:
Enter SECOND Digit

↓

Switch all 3 lights
OFF

↓

1, 5, 6 ⚡ ← FALSE ADD [the number of lights switched 'ON']

↓

Are all 3 lights ON? —No→ Switch ON one additional light

Yes
↓

The Initial Digit
Entered was Correct

lights

- If you hit a lightning box, and the number's value is shown in the box, sadly the robot is electrocuted and breaks down, which means the number is incorrect.

- If you hit a FALSE ADD box, then change the current value by that amount (though your START number remains the same, and is still the number that should be part of the code)

- Your number cannot be more than 10, so for any number above 10 subtract 10. This means 9+3 = 2, rather than 12

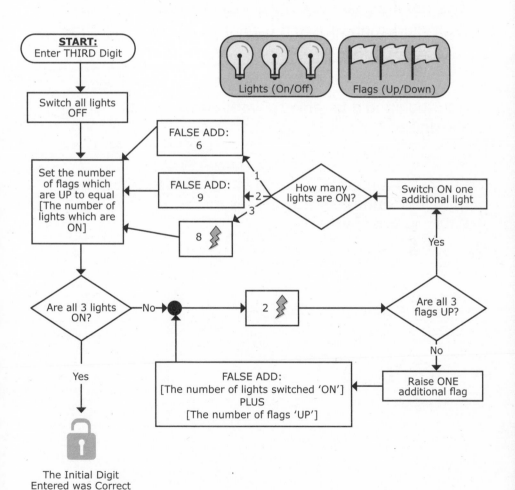

LANGUAGES

Rose

Esperanto is a language that's been created so it has simple grammar and spelling rules, which makes it easier to learn. We know that the leader has been learning Esperanto, and used it to disguise the code for opening the deposit box.

You too should be able to work out the rules just from looking at the sheet opposite.

We found a message with a code for the deposit box:
Kvincent dudek kvar mil cent dudek.
What number is that?

Amount	English	Esperanto
Eggs in half a dozen		ses
Squares on a noughts and crosses grid		naŭ
Tentacles on an octopus		ok
Horns on a unicorn		unu
Nostrils in a nose		du
Number of deadly sins		sep
Wings on a dragonfly		kvar
X, to a Roman		dek
Legs on a snake		nulo
Number of Olympic rings		kvin
Legs on a tripod		tri
One dozen		dek du
Playing cards in a suit		dek tri
Number at the top of a dartboard		dudek
Miles in a marathon		dudek ses
Playing cards in a deck		kvindek du
Squares on a chess board		sesdek kvar
Years in a century		cent
A dozen dozens		cent kvardek kvar
Days in a year		tricent sesdek kvin
Seconds in an hour		tri mil sescent
Inches in a mile		sesdek tri mil tricent sesdek

CYBER SECURITY

Sandeep

We need to know the password for the laptop in the deposit box. We've recovered a folder which we think contains clues to the password. In it are a map and some post-it notes. Could these be clues to the password? Can you work out what it is?

ICELAND

FAEROES

IRELAND

?

NCSC Password Advice

one
Use ~~three~~ random words

~~GREAT~~

_ _ _ _ _ _

Aide-memoire!

Battle 19:40

Festival 19:51

Finally, we need to find which city the suspects have chosen for their dastardly plot!

We've intercepted a grid from suspect C, but it's missing some information which they think only the other suspects know . . . the answers to the previous puzzles in this section.

Colin

But we have some things they weren't counting on. The power of teamwork. Help Colin, Rose, Shanti, Meg, Riley, Elizabeth, Greg and Sandeep: in the grid on the last page of the colour section, solve the clues underneath it and cross them off, then read what's left so that we can get to the bank before it's too late.

Good Luck!

Additional answer spaces

Codebreaking (RED): _ _ _ _ _ _ _

Maths (ORANGE): _ _

Engineering (YELLOW): _ _ _ _ _ _ _ _

Coding (GREEN): _ _ _

Languages (LIGHT BLUE): _ _ _ _ _ _

Cyber Security (PURPLE): _ _ _ _ _ _ _

Analysis (PINK): _ _ _ _ _ _

Answers

ANSWERS: GETTING STARTED

1 The early bird

LEOTARD is **LEOPARD**

DECK is **DUCK**

WOLD is **WOLF**

BOX is **FOX**

PEG is **PIG**

SHAKE is **SNAKE**

When you spell out
the missing letters,
you get PUFFIN!

2 Cryptic calendar

4 JULY
The months follow in calendar order, so July will be next
after June.

You can find the exact date by looking at the number of
letters in each month. For instance, February has eight
letters, so is **8 February**, March five letters, so is **5 March**.
And July has four letters, which must mean it's **4 July.**

The answer to the second part of the question is the **United
States of America.**

3 Food for thought

STEWARD contains **STEW**

OCTONION contains **ONION**

TRICERATOPS contains **RICE**

BUNNY contains **BUN**

BEGGAR contains **EGG**

JUMPSTART contains **TART**

The dessert
is SORBET!

4 Microdot-to-microdot

The lines between the dots spell out **GCHQ.**

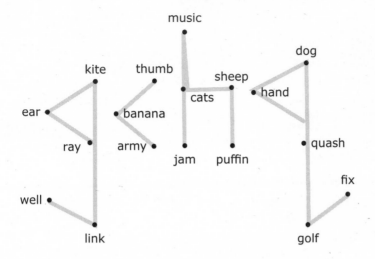

5 Excellent Entertaining Limerick

The first letter of each line in the limerick spells out **TROUT** – which is the answer!

6 Frankenstein's wordsearch

You can find EAR, ELBOW, EYE, FOOT, HAND, JAW, LEG, NOSE, SHIN, TOE and TUMMY.

In the third row, you can also find the word TAIL. This is the only word in the grid which isn't a part of the human body.

T	O	O	F	W	L
E	N	H	R	A	E
L	I	A	T	J	G
B	H	N	O	S	E
O	S	D	E	Y	E
W	Y	M	M	U	T

7 Mini crossword

	¹B		²C		³M
⁴M	A	T	A	T	A
	N		N		L
⁵P	A	N	A	M	A
	N		D		L
⁶S	A	H	A	R	A

Did you spot the connection between the answers? In each word, every other letter is an A, which might have helped you complete the crossword!

8 Fishing expedition

If you draw lines between the end of the rods and the fishes' mouths, it spells out TAXI.

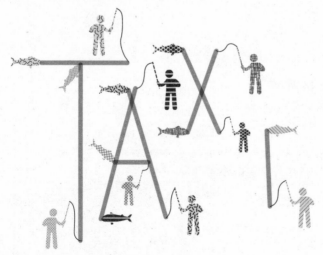

This is how they all got home!

9 Richard of York

a) **RANGE – RED, O**RANGE**, YELLOW, GREEN, BLUE, INDIGO, VIOLET**

b) **ART – MERCURY, VENUS, EAR**T**H, MARS, JUPITER, SATURN, URANUS, NEPTUNE**

c) **DEW –** MON**DAY,** TUE**S**DAY, WED**NES**DAY, THU**RS**DAY, FRI**DAY,** SAT**URDAY,** SUN**DAY**

(The sequence is the first three letters of each day written backwards.)

10 Burn me

These are all anagrams of numbers:

HERD UNDONE	**ONE HUNDRED**
HIT ENTER	**THIRTEEN**
IFFY TETHER	**FIFTY THREE**
THY TWEETING	**TWENTY EIGHT**
TIN YEN	**NINETY**
TWIX TOYS	**SIXTY TWO**
TYNE ROOF	**FORTY ONE**
WITTY THOR	**THIRTY TWO**
YES VENT	**SEVENTY**
YOU FIGHTER	**EIGHTY FOUR**

So the answer is to put them in numerical order, with **HIT ENTER** (thirteen) first, and **HERD UNDONE** (one hundred) last.

Even the question title is an anagram. If you rearrange the letters in **BURN ME**, you can get the word **NUMBER**.

11 A-maze-ing challenge

12 Animal-agram

a) Six words that are anagrams of animals:

BARGED – **BADGER**

BOLSTER – **LOBSTER**

HEAR – **HARE**

HEROS – **HORSE**

LEOPARD – **PAROLED**

SWAP – **WASP**

b) Six words that can have one letter changed to give the name of an animal:

BRAVER – **BEAVER**

CAMEO – **CAMEL**

HEAR – **BEAR**

HEROS – **HERON**

MUFFIN – **PUFFIN**

SWAP – **SWAN**

c) Which means that these three words fit into both categories:

HEAR   HEROS   SWAP

13 Odd one in

a) HOUSE is the odd one out, as it's the only one that's not a fruit.

b) STRAWBERRY is the odd one out, as it's the only one that doesn't start with the letter P.

c) GOOSEBERRY is the odd one out, as the rest each have five letters.

d) TANGERINE is the odd one out, as it's the only one that doesn't end with the letter T.

e) GLOUCESTER is the only word not beginning with W. **WARRINGTON** is the only word not ending with ER. **WOODPECKER** is a bird and not a town or city. **WORCESTER** is only 9 letters while the other words are 10 letters.

Therefore, **WINCHESTER** is the only one which isn't the odd one out – so it is the odd one in!

14 The right key

The answers are:

a) BAG

b) FEED

c) DECADE

d) CAGE

e) BABBAGE. This final question was a tough one! Charles Babbage was a mathematician and inventor, who is widely thought to have invented the first digital computer.

15 The serpent

The letters in grey spell out
CROSSWORD.

16 Bird brain

The six birds you can find are:

PEAHEN

PELICAN

PENGUIN

PIGEON

PTARMIGAN

PUFFIN

For each bird, it's possible to travel through the maze by only going through each letter (in order) once. Did you manage to do it?

17 Maze message

Below is the maze with the featured words shaded in. By identifying and avoiding the obstacles (the shaded words), you can find a path through the maze, where the middle letter '**H**' in **ARCHWAY** is the starting point.

E	H	F	U	O	Y	Y	A	Y
G	E	O	T	E	R	F	R	A
A	D	U	A	F	I	A	O	W
S	G	N	W	F	L	L	O	H
S	E	D	T	H	C	L	G	C
E	M	P	O	E	W	B	O	R
I	T	D	N	S	A	E	S	A
N	E	R	C	E	L	V	B	E
S	E	C	T	S	L	I	H	E

Reading the text along the path from start to finish, the message is revealed:

HOORAY YOU FOUND THE SECRET MESSAGE.

18 Spot-the-difference – animal edition

The two missing birds are **FLAMINGO** and **COCKEREL**.

The coordinates for the differences on each square correspond to the letters which spell out each bird. For instance, the rhino's horn (missing on one diagram but present on another) has the coordinates F (on the vertical side) and L (on the horizontal side). The stripes on the lemur's tale (which have more on one diagram than another) correspond to the letters A and M. And so on.

The number of differences in each square will show you the order the letters should go in.

19 Tea and snake

HOUSE NUMBER	NAME	DRINK	PET
1	Wesley	Hot Choc	Otter
2	Hassan	Apple Juice	Snake
3	Tia	Earl Grey	Alligator

Here's how you might have been able to work it out:

You know that Hassan must live at house number 2, as he has two neighbours. That means Tia lives at house number 3, and Wesley at house number 1. The snake lives at an even number, so that must be house 2, with Hassan. We know that Wesley doesn't own an alligator, so that must belong to Tia. Wesley, the otter owner, must therefore drink hot chocolate. Because the apple juice drinker lives to the left of the Earl Grey drinker, that must mean Hassan drinks apple juice, and Tia drinks Earl Grey!

If you look at the first letter of each answer, from left to right, heading down the table, it spells out WHO HAS TEA.
So the answer to the hidden question is Tia!

20 At sixes and sevens

The paired words are listed below. You'll notice that the right-hand list is in **alphabetical order**. The linked word to LAMB must be SHEEP. If you also put SHEEP in alphabetical order in the right-hand list, then LAMB must go between HEPTAGON and HEXAGON in the left-hand list.

WORD	LINKED WORD
FORWARD	BACKWARD
BRUSSELS	BELGIUM
KITTEN	CAT
CALF	COW
PUPPY	DOG
UP	DOWN
OCTAGON	EIGHT
PENTAGON	FIVE
SQUARE	FOUR
PARIS	FRANCE
BERLIN	GERMANY
KID	GOAT
FOAL	HORSE
ROME	ITALY
IN	OUT
LISBON	PORTUGAL
LEFT	RIGHT
HEPTAGON	SEVEN
LAMB	SHEEP
HEXAGON	SIX
MADRID	SPAIN
TRIANGLE	THREE
BOTTOM	TOP
OVER	UNDER

ANSWERS: LANGUAGES

1 Cracking packing

There are a few different ways to get from the top to the bottom of each lock, but here are some of the most straightforward.

TOP – **H**OP – HO**T** – H**A**T

FAST – **C**AST – CAS**E** – CA**N**E – **L**ANE

GOOD – GO**L**D – **T**OLD – TOL**L** -TI**L**L – TIL**E** – TIME

2 First stop

a) The cat is in the house.
   Le chat est dans la maison.
b) The dog is in the garden.
   Le chien est dans le jardin.

3 From Paris to Berlin

a) Glove
b) Umbrella
c) Vet
d) Plane

4 Going Dutch

a) Three books
b) Seven children
c) Eight shoes
d) Two animals

5 Ancient lingo

GREEK		ENGLISH
ΑΦΡΟΔΙΤΗ	=	APHRODITE
ΓΗ	=	GAIA
ΑΡΗΣ	=	ARES
ΖΕΥΣ	=	ZEUS
ΚΡΟΝΟΣ	=	KRONOS
ΟΥΡΑΝΟΣ	=	OURANOS
ΠΟΣΕΙΔΩΝΑΣ	=	POSEIDONAS
ΣΕΛΗΝΗ	=	SELENE
ΠΛΟΥΤΩΝΑΣ	=	PLUOTONAS

6 Chatting in Arabic

a) Ismi

a) Ismha

a) how are you? = Kayf al-Hal?.

sad = Hazin, excellent = mumtaz

7 Flying to Japan

Here is what the wordsearch looks like with all the hiragana words in the question highlighted:

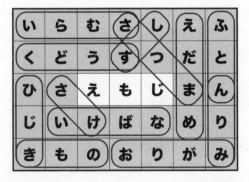

You can see that the three remaining hiragana are え (e), も (mo) and じ (ji).

Put these together and you get **emoji**, which is a very modern language!

8 It's time for Africa

a) takwas

b) biyar

c) (goma) sha ɗaya

d) tara

e) shida

f) (goma) sha shida

g) (goma) sha takwas

h) ishirin da biyu
   (or ashirin da biyu)

i) arba'in

j) ishirin da bakwai
   (or ashirin da bakwai)

k) talatin da huɗu

l) casa'in da tara

m) hamsin da shida

9 Yes you Afrikaan!

Directions:

AFRIKAANS	ENGLISH
Noord	North
Wes	West
Oos	East
Suid	South

Numbers:

AFRIKAANS	ENGLISH
Vyf	Five
Ses	Six
Agt	Eight
Drie	Three
Een	One
Tien	Ten
Twee	Two
Ver	Four
Nege	Nine
Sewe	Seven

Here is the completed chart:

DIRECTION	ENGLISH	NUMBER OF SQUARES	ENGLISH	PLACE	LAST LETTER
oos	*east*	drie	3	*park*	k
suid	*south*	nege	9	*sauna*	a
wes	*west*	twee	2	*cinema*	a
noord	*north*	vyf	5	*bus stop*	p
oos	*east*	vier	4	*butcher's*	s
noord	*north*	een	1	*forest*	t
suid	*south*	ses	6	*spa*	a
wes	*west*	drie	3	*pond*	d

The last letters spell out kaapstad, which is **Cape Town**, in Afrikaans.

10 Numero diez

Here is the table, with the blanks filled in and in bold:

the house	la casa
the houses	las casas
my house	mi casa
your house	tu casa
our house	nuestra casa
the bicycle	la bicicleta
your bicycles	tus bicicletas
my bicycle	**mi bicicleta**
our tickets	nuestras entradas
the tickets	**las entradas**
my job	mi trabajo

my sister	mi hermana
your sister	tu hermana
our sisters	**nuestras hermanas**
our brother	nuestro hermano
my sisters	mis hermanas
our English grandmother	nuestra abuela inglesa
your grandfathers	tus abuelos
our English house	nuestra casa inglesa
your brothers	**tus hermanos**
your English bicycle	**tu bicicleta inglesa**
our jobs	**nuestros trabajos**
your grandmothers	**tu abuelas**

11 Chill in Chile!

ENGLISH	SPANISH
Right	Derecha
Left	Izquierda
Building	Edificio
Street	Calle
Take	Toma

ENGLISH	SPANISH
First	Primer/Primera
Second	Segunda/Segundo
Third	Tercer/Tercera
Turn	Gira/Giro
Pass	Pase

This was a really tricky one! You need to have used the Spanish you learned from the first example, and added to the table, to work out the destinations. For instance, because you know certain words, you can work out the first sentence of the directions for the first destination like so:

Gira a la izquierda [left] **por la calle** [street] **y toma la primera** [first] **a la derecha** [right].

Filling the gaps, you can work out that the instructions are telling you to turn left down the street, and take the first right.

Try doing this for the other directions if you weren't able to work it out on the first go.

Destinations:

First destination – **location 13, Casa Museo Max Moreau**
Second destination – **location 21, Barracudas**
Third destination – **location 16, Teatro Real**

12 Finishing in style

Braille	City
⠿	London
⠿	Paris
⠿	Berlin
⠿	The Hague
⠿	Lisbon
⠿	Madrid
⠿	Prague
⠿	Vienna
⠿	Sarajevo
⠿	Copenhagen
⠿	Zagreb
⠿	Reykjavik
⠿	Rome
⠿	Minsk

ANSWERS: ENGINEERING

STEP 1 Fresh out of the box

Shapes 1 and 7 combine to form A

Shapes 2, 3 and 6 combine to form B

Shapes 4, 5 and 8 combine to form C

STEP 2 Grand designs

Only Robot 2 answers all the requirements:

- It needs more wheels than arms. (Rules out 1.)
- Speed is more important than strength. (Rules out 1.)
- Night vision would be nice but not essential.
  (Doesn't rule out any of the robots.)
- Battery life needs to be at least as good as strength.
  (Rules out 3.)

STEP 3 Side by side

B – Looking at the robot from the side, you would
only be able to see one leg and one arm.

STEP 4 Prototype

SHAPE	QUANTITY
A	1
B	6
C	4
D	1

STEP 5 Ronnie, Romy and Rowan

Robot 1: **Rowan**   Robot 2: **Ronnie**   Robot 3: **Romy**

Robot 1 has the least shapes AND the least total pieces of all three robots, so can't be Romy or Ronnie, and must be Rowan.

Now it's easy to work out which of the other two has a greater number of different shapes than the other (Robot 2: Ronnie) and which has more shapes in total (Robot 3: Romy).

STEP 6 Missing parts

You have enough shapes to build **Robots 1** and **3**.

This is because there are only two squares, which means you can't build Robots 2 and 3 (you'd need three squares in total). And there are only four rectangles, which means you can't build Robots 1 and 2 (you'd need five rectangles in total).

STEP 7 The cogs are turning

A will turn anticlockwise.
B will turn clockwise.

STEP 8 Crossed wires

There are eight mistakes to find. The arrows show how you can fix these in five steps.

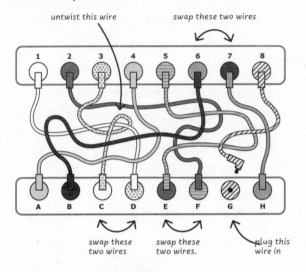

untwist this wire

swap these two wires

swap these two wires

swap these two wires.

plug this wire in

STEP 9 Circuit breaker

Here is how the pieces fit together.

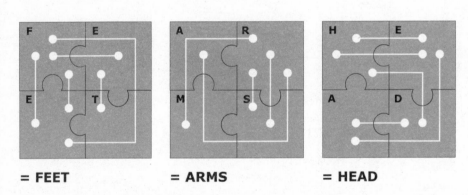

= FEET   = ARMS   = HEAD

There is a hidden answer for this question! Did you spot how, when the letters for each board are put together, they spell out different robot parts?!

STEP 10 Robot race

Fourteen days is the quickest time it will take the team to build the robot.

Here is a diagram showing how you might have been able to work it out:

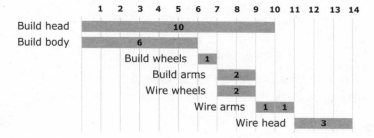

STEP 11 Power up

Battery B and **Motor C**.

This is the only combination of battery and motor which means the battery has enough voltage for the motor – and the combined weight of the battery, motor and robot won't be too great!

STEP 12 Repair shop

The following moves will enable you to move all the components to slot 2.

MOVE 1   A goes to slot 3

MOVE 2   B goes to slot 2

MOVE 3   A goes to slot 2

MOVE 4   C goes to slot 3

MOVE 5   A goes to slot 1

MOVE 6   B goes to slot 3

MOVE 7   A goes to slot 3

MOVE 8   D goes to slot 2

MOVE 9   A goes to slot 2

MOVE 10   B goes to slot 1

MOVE 11   A goes to slot 1

MOVE 12   C goes to slot 2

MOVE 13   A goes to slot 3

MOVE 14   B goes to slot 2

MOVE 15   A goes to slot 2

STEP 13 On the move

The correct order for the moves is:

1. RUUR   **5.** URDR

2. RUUL   **6.** DRUR

3. URRU   **7.** URDR

4. LULU   **8.** RRUR

To find the password, take the letter for each move, and if you place them in the order the moves should go in, it spells out: **LEARNING**.

STEP 14 Chips are down

a) **ELECTRICAL**
MECHANICAL
SOFTWARE

b) **RO BO TS AR EA WE SO ME**
(ROBOTS ARE AWESOME)

STEP 15 On the right track

The letters in the code correspond to a compass:

N = North, S = South, E = East, W = West

The number following the letter corresponds to how many squares in that direction (N, S, E, W) the robot should travel. For example, N10 means: travel north for ten squares. E2 means: travel east for two squares.

The other letters correspond to obstacles on the map:

T = Tunnel, and is an instruction to the robot to travel through the tunnel.

B = Bridge, and is an instruction to the robot to travel over the bridge.

Semi-colons are used to separate each individual instruction.

Journey 3: The robot's destination is the **shop**.

Journey 4: The robot must start at the **bus station**, and end at the **friend's house**.

Journey 5: There are many routes you could take. Here is one of them:

Travel south for 16 squares = **S16**

Travel east for 1 square = **E1**

Travel south for 4 squares = **S4**

Travel over the bridge = **B**

Travel south for 5 squares = **S5**

Travel east for 6 squares = **E6**

Travel south for 7 squares = **S7**

Answer: **S16; E1; S4; B; S5; E6; S7**

STEP 16 Power off

The correct code is **6739**

ANSWERS: CODEBREAKING

1 Your first code – as easy as BCD

a) LEARNING ABOUT CODES IS FUN

b) CREATING CODES IS FUNNER!

c) BREAKING CODES IS FUNNEST!

d) NOW IT'S TIME TO TRY SOME HARDER CODES

2 Introducing . . . code blocks

a) 8X76

b) ROCKET

c) A SECRET MESSAGE

3 Introducing . . . a key

a) DBCF

b) COMET

c) ANOTHER SECRET MESSAGE

d) KILLER WHALE

e) WELCOME TO JURASSIC PARK

V	E	L	O	C	I	R	A	P
D	F	G	H	J	K	M	N	T
B	Z	Y	X	W	U	S	Q	1
0	9	8	7	6	5	4	3	2

4 Patterns and guesses: cribs and collateral

a) BANANA

b) NEPTUNE

5 One and the same

a) LIME

b) JANUARY

c) ORANGE

d) WE SHOULD COMMUNICATE IN CODE SO THAT NOBODY CAN READ OUR MESSAGES

6 The Enigma method

a) HEADS

b) FRIDAY

c) GEMINI

d) SIX is greater than FOUR

7 Reconstructing a code block

a) MONDAY 8TH FEBRUARY NOTHING TO REPORT

b) TUESDAY 9TH FEBRUARY NOTHING TO REPORT

c) WARTHOG

W	A	R	T	H	O	G	1	2
F	I	J	K	L	M	N	P	3
E	Z	Y	X	V	U	S	Q	4
D	C	B	0	9	8	7	6	5

8 Puzzling polygons

By counting the sides of each shape, this gives you the code word: **362753**.

Using the keyword, this deciphers to **SHAPES**.

9 Catch of the day

The lobsters and crabs can be found as follows:

The spare letters can be read left-to-right, top-to-bottom to spell the answer: **BLETCHLEY PARK**.

For very observant puzzlers, there is a hidden answer in this question. The letters at the top of the T in each lobster spell out the phrase **KEY IS KNOX**.

K	N	O	X	1	2	3	4	5
H	I	J	L	M	P	Q	R	6
G	Z	Y	W	V	U	T	S	7
F	E	D	C	B	A	0	9	8

You can use this key to decipher the letters in the centre of the crabs, which is **WDSNEI**. This deciphers to **LORENZ**, which was the name of the machine used by Germany to create codes during the Second World War.

10 Bletchley Park – Hut 8

The message reads **UNUSED LETTERS KEY IS NAVY**.

The unused letters are: **VPSHTGFNV**. Using a code block with the key NAVY, this can be decrypted to **ESPIONAGE**.

N	A	V	Y	1	2	3	4	5
I	J	K	L	M	O	P	Q	6
H	Z	X	W	U	T	S	R	7
G	F	E	D	C	B	0	9	8

ANSWERS: ANALYSIS

1 Look who's talking

Suspect A – Laptop
Suspect B – Games console
Suspect C – Tablet
Suspect D – Phone
Suspect E – PC

2 Notebook clues

E was the suspect who was met with most times.
• A was met with seven times
• B was met with seven times
• D was met with six times
• E was met with eight times

3 Spinning a web

a) Here is the route
Suspect D took:

b) Suspect A
could have
taken two
routes.

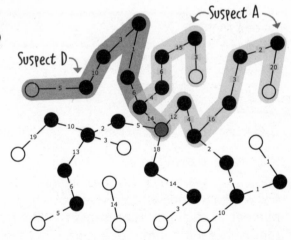

4 The magic number
+447700901396 is the only number that matches all the
information given.

5 Lock and key

The numbers are in alphabetical order, so the missing ones are:

8 – 5 – **4** – 9 – **1** – **7** – 6 – **3** – 2 – 0

6 Profile puzzle

The suspects are **a, b, e, g, j**

7 Work patterns

a) They didn't come in on Thursday 17th.

b) They left the office on Tuesday 15th between 11:35 and 12:01.

c) On Wednesday 9th, they exited the office at 18:04 (34 mins overstay).
On Friday 18th they entered the office at 07:22 (38 mins early).

d) The theft took place on Friday 18th from 07:22 to 08:00, when the suspect had 38 minutes alone in the office.

8 Botanical brainteaser

Suspect D is flying to Berlin and then Prague.

The pairs of numbers refer to specific letters in the text from the book, which when written down give you the locations. The first number in each pair represents the line number, and the second represents the number of letters it is along that line.

Put together, this spells out BERLIN for the first location.
The same approach to the second location then tells you they are going to EUGARP. The R suggests you need to reverse it get the answer: PRAGUE.

9 Briefcase password

The password is **TESTING**.

Q	X	Y	M	O	R	H
T	E	S	T	I	N	G
Right of Q	**Below X**	**Above Y**	**Right of M**	**Left of O**	**Above R**	**Left of H**

10 Phone call conundrum

The suspect on the phone is an author. This is suspect C, who lives in Manchester and speaks Swedish. The other suspects are A, who is a teacher who speaks French and lives in Scarborough; B, who is a banker who speaks Italian and lives in London; and D, who is an engineer who speaks German and lives in Cheltenham.

11 Needle in a haystack

The number 5 on the envelope is a hint to look at every fifth letter along (and the 'ignore space' tells you to ignore the space between the words as you count).

FROG **L**ION T**O**AD CE**N**TAUR **D**OG SL**O**TH HE**N**

Reading every fifth letter spells out **London**, which shows you where Suspect D will be hiding.

12 Which receipt?

- A – receipt 3
- B – receipt 4
- C – receipt 2
- D – receipt 5
- E – receipt 1

Here is how you can work this one out:

- Receipt 5 includes chewing gum and goldfish food, so must belong to someone who chews gum and also owns a pet. This can only be Suspect D.

- Receipt 4 includes bubblegum, so must belong to one of the remaining gum chewers: Suspects B and E. It also includes peanuts though, so it can't belong to Suspect E who has a nut allergy. Therefore it belongs to Suspect B.

- Receipt 3 includes a dog toy so must belong to one of the remaining pet owners: Suspect A or C. It also contains bacon, so it can't belong to Suspect C, who is vegetarian. Therefore it belongs to Suspect A.

- That only leaves Suspects C and E. Receipt 2 contains a Snickers bar, so can't belong to Suspect E. Therefore it belongs to Suspect C, and hence receipt 1 must belong to Suspect E.

- The fact that Suspect A doesn't like fizzy drinks, or that some receipts include vegetarian food, is not needed to solve the problem.

13 Follow the leader

F is not in charge, Suspect D is.

This is because Suspect D talks to everyone. F only talks to Suspects D, A and B.

If you were to draw a diagram of who talks to who, it would show Suspect D at the centre, and Suspect F, Suspect A and Suspect B would be a separate group who talk to each other, with Suspects C and E as another separate group. We call these separate groups **subgroups**.

ANSWERS: MATHEMATICS

1 The foundations of mathematics

SEC	OND	MIN	UTE	HO	UR	D	AY	WE	EK
		ON	E	TE	N	HUN	DRED	THOU	SAND
WHO	LE	HA	LF	TH	IRD	QUAR	TER	FIF	TH
		PO	INT	LI	NE	SH	APE	SOL	ID
CIR	CLE	CRES	CENT	TRIA	NGLE	SQU	ARE	PENT	AGON
	A	DD	DIV	IDE	MULT	IPLY	SUBT	RACT	
O	NE	T	WO	TH	REE	F	OUR	FI	VE

2 Six-in-one

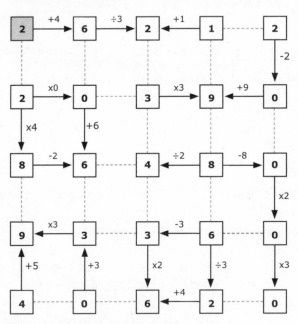

3 What the Romans did for us

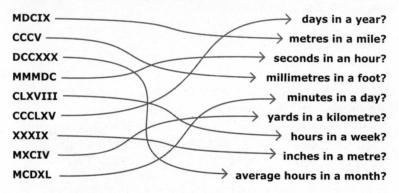

MDCIX   → days in a year?
CCCV   → metres in a mile?
DCCXXX   → seconds in an hour?
MMMDC   → millimetres in a foot?
CLXVIII   → minutes in a day?
CCCLXV   → yards in a kilometre?
XXXIX   → hours in a week?
MXCIV   → inches in a metre?
MCDXL   → average hours in a month?

X	X	X	I	X	I
V	X	M	C	M	I
L	X	X	V	X	I
X	C	L	I	I	V
D	C	C	C	V	X
C	D	X	X	C	L
M	M	M	M	D	C

The remaining letters, read in order, are MCMXIX, which is the year 1919, when GC&CS (now GCHQ) was founded.

4 Game, Set, Matchstick

a) You move a matchstick in the 2, to make it into a 3.

$$2 + 5 = 8 \qquad 3 + 5 = 8$$

b) You move a matchstick from the 8 to the 9, to make them 6 and 8 respectively.

$$9 - 8 = 2 \qquad 8 - 6 = 2$$

c) You move a matchstick from the 8 to the 3, to make them 0 and 9 respectively.

$$6 - 5 = 8 \qquad 6 - 6 = 0$$

d) You move a matchstick from the 8 to the 5, to make them 0 and 6 respectively.

$$8 + 5 = 6 \qquad 0 + 6 = 6$$

e) You move a matchstick from the + to the 6, making them − and 8 respectively.

$$6 + 3 = 5 \qquad 8 - 3 = 5$$

f) You move a matchstick from the 6, to form a − in front of the 4.

$$4 + 9 = 6 \qquad -4 + 9 = 5$$

5 Filling in the Caps

a) ELEVEN (11) is the number that uses only straight lines when written in digits or as a word. (The only digits available are 1, 4 and 7; but any number containing a 4 contains the letter O, and any number containing a 7 contains the letter S. We can only avoid using the O in ONE by using the number 11.)

b) FIVE (5) is the smallest number that has no enclosed spaces when written as a word or in digits. (Each of ONE, TWO, THREE and FOUR contains either an O or an R.)

c) SEVENTY-SEVEN (77) is the largest such number. (We cannot use the digits 8 or 9, and no number above 100 will work either.)

6 Elevenses

1 (ONE) is the first number written with three letters.

4 (FOUR) is the first number written with four letters.

3 (THREE) is the first number written with five letters.

11 (ELEVEN) is the first number written with six letters.

To continue the pattern, we need the first number written with eleven letters: this is **23 (TWENTY-THREE)**.

7 Letters and numbers

a) A=5, B=1

b) A=50, B=5, C=2, D=8

c) A=7, B=3, C=2, D=5

d) A=27, B=26, C=30, D=15, E=12, F=18, G=16, H=25

8 Buried treasure

To get the answer, you need to take the coordinates from the horizontal axis on the map, and then the vertical axis, and put them in the order of where the sailor stopped.

Our first location gives us (G,R), our second location is (E,Y), then (J,U), followed by (M,P) and then (E,R). If we put these together, we get GREY JUMPER.

9 Mixed-up sums

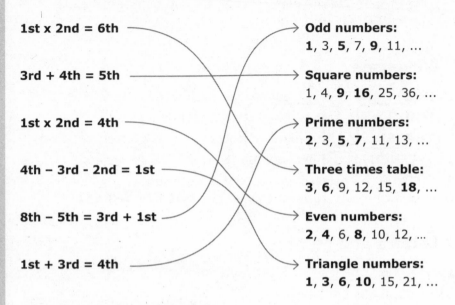

1st x 2nd = 6th → Odd numbers:
1, 3, **5**, 7, **9**, 11, ...

3rd + 4th = 5th → Square numbers:
1, 4, **9**, **16**, 25, 36, ...

1st x 2nd = 4th → Prime numbers:
2, 3, **5**, **7**, 11, 13, ...

4th − 3rd - 2nd = 1st → Three times table:
3, **6**, 9, 12, 15, **18**, ...

8th − 5th = 3rd + 1st → Even numbers:
2, **4**, 6, **8**, 10, 12, ...

1st + 3rd = 4th → Triangle numbers:
1, **3**, **6**, **10**, 15, 21, ...

10 The magic number

a) 49   **b)** 57   **c)** 816

11 Crossing in Königsberg

Bridge **b)** is the actual plan of Königsberg. In the other plans,
each of the bridges can be crossed in a single walk as follows:

a)

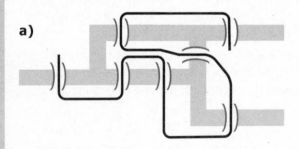

b)

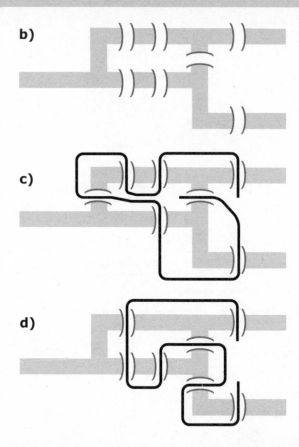

c)

d)

What Euler realised was that you have to consider how many bridges have an end in each separate area of land. If there are two areas with an odd number of bridge-ends, then you need to start in one and end in the other to complete your walk. If there are more than two such areas, then it isn't possible to do the walk. In the real Königsberg, you can see that there are three bridge-ends above the river in the diagram and three below. The little island has five and the area of land on the right has three. The reason for this is that to complete a walk you have to leave an area as often as you reach it, except for where you start and where you end.

Note that Bridge d is the only one that can start and end at the same place. This is because it is the only one where all the areas have an even number of bridge-ends.

12 Padlock pairs

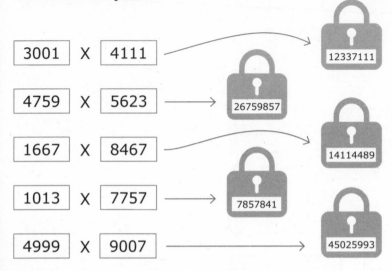

3001	X	4111	→	12337111
4759	X	5623	→	26759857
1667	X	8467	→	14114489
1013	X	7757	→	7857841
4999	X	9007	→	45025993

13 Crack the safe

a) This is an even number, so is a multiple of 2:
   992102 = 2 x 496051

b) This ends with 5, so is a multiple of 5:
   861395 = 5 x 172279

c) Trying other small numbers, we find that:
   700021 = 7 x 100003

14 Feeling confident?

a) The square root of 67765823 is just under 8232,
   so trying the numbers either side of this shows that:
   67765823 = 8231 x 8233

b) Similarly square rooting 64160099 suggests:
   64160099 = 8009 x 8011

c) And square rooting 80999999 suggests trying:
   80999999 = 8999 x 9001

ANSWERS: CODING

1 Missed connections

a) E

b) B

c) 13

d) Yes - RAIL to E, BOAT to A, FLY to Y

e) Y

2 Vend-a-hand, please!

a) Apple

b) Doughnut

c) Banana

d) Eccles cake and banana

e) An Eccles cake, £1, a chocolate bar and an apple

3 Difficult dataflow

a) Subtraction

b) 1 + 2 = 3; 7 − 3 = 4; 3 x 4 = 12

c) 3 x 3 = 9; 9 − 2 = 7 (which then has 2 added to it, so goes back to 9); 9 + 9 = 18

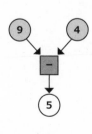

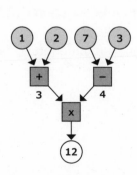

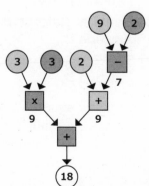

4 Fun functions

C, A, B

5 Dog days

a) Triangle (to B), circle (to F), circle (to J), circle (to I), circle (to J)

b) No. If you cannot say 'triangle' then there is no way to get to platforms B/D/F, so you cannot visit B as needed.

c) No. If you cannot say 'circle' then there is no way to get to the final platform J.

d) One solution is triangle, triangle (dogs 1 and 3 are now together on A), circle, triangle (all three dogs are now on D), square, circle.

6 Have you got what it takes?

a) Sign 3 will split the pair, as Bob's first digit is even, whereas Alice's is not.

b) Sign 3 at Junction B will separate off Ed (as his first digit is even) to the Ada Lovelace room. And then using Sign 1 at Junction D will separate Charlie and Dani (as their numbers are below and above 5000 respectively).

c) Sign 3 will send Bob and Ed to one room, Charlie and Dani to another.

d) Sign 3 at Junction B; Sign 4 at Junction C; Sign 1 at Junction D.

e) Sign 3 at Junction A; Sign 1 at Junction B; Sign 2 at Junction D.

7 It's in the net

a) Add IS should read Add NIS

b) A=2; B=4; C=1 ; D=3

c) A=3 (to give CROCKET); B=2 (to give HOCKET); C=1 (to give HOCKEY as required)

8 Tommy's Flowers

The flowers should be arranged as follows:

tulip, dahlia, rose, tulip, rose, dahlia, rose, tulip

9 You only move twice

a) Play CARD 2 to move two hexes to C1. Then play CARD 1 to move three spaces to A3/helicopter.

b) Play CARD 4 to add one to CARD 3 and move the satellite dish two hexes to D2 (next to player and just above the police officer). Then play CARD 1 to move three hexes to E5. Then CARD 2 to move the final two hexes to the seaplane on E7.

ANSWERS: CYBER SECURITY

1 Word decoder

[1] TABLETS   **[2]** CYBER SECURITY

[3] COMPUTERS   **[4]** INTRUSIONS

[5] SMARTPHONES   **[6]** CYBER ATTACKS

[7] NATIONAL CYBER SECURITY CENTRE

[8] LAPTOPS   **[9]** INTERNET

2 Logging on

Only RainBallMango would make a strong password.
Cyber criminals who want to find a password usually
look for patterns, therefore option **a)** is too predictable
by using all the seasons and option **b)** is such a common
password it is easily guessable.

3 A safe password

a) Password

b) Liverpool

c) Security

d) Spiderman

e) Disneyland

4 Guess the password

a) UpTheGunners07

b) 1et1tg0

c) Sk8rGirl

d) Labrador1010

5 Safety is key

Amy uses text messaging on the phone.
Beth chooses to use an authentication app on the laptop.
Mina uses a fingerprint reader on the tablet.

6 Backing up

Reading down the grid
are types of data you
might want to back up:

EMAIL
VIDEOS
PHOTOS
HOMEWORK
MESSAGES
MUSIC

Reading back
up is advice:

**COPY THINGS THAT
YOU VALUE ONTO A
DIFFERENT DEVICE**

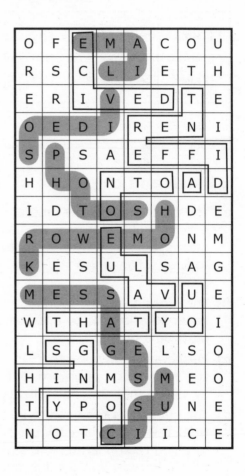

7 New starters

NAME	ROLE	PERMISSIONS
River	Doctor	VIEW and EDIT MEDICAL records ONLY
Zahra	Paramedic	VIEW MEDICAL records ONLY
Zeke	Receptionist	CREATE and EDIT PERSONAL records ONLY
Lou	Patient	VIEW PERSONAL and MEDICAL records ONLY

8 Phish and chips

a) The email address the message is from includes **glocester**, which is not the correct spelling of the bank's name. This means it can't be from the actual bank. The email asks you to open a file, which you shouldn't as you don't trust the sender.

b) The email is asking Charlie to send his password. That would never be asked for by a legitimate company, so the message must be a fake.

c) Phishers can be persistent! In this case, not only are they still asking for a password, but they are applying pressure by saying that criminals will act in the next 24 hours.

d) The offer looks too good to be true – so it probably isn't true! The sender is really urging Charlie to click on the link by using capital letters and saying that only the first fifty people to reply will get the cheap tickets. This email may have gone to all the fan-club members, and the phishers will be happy even if only one or two people fall for it.

9 Cyber search

The words in the grid are:
TECHNOLOGY, IMPORTANT, MILITARY, NATIONAL, SHOPPING, PROTECT, THREATS, GAMING, ONLINE, SOCIAL, ARMED, CYBER, MEDIA, MONEY, FORCE and **FAKE NEWS.**

The remaining letters spell **PARTNERSHIP**.

Y	E	N	O	M	F	O	R	C	E
S	G	A	M	I	N	G	P	N	I
W	S	O	I	M	E	D	I	A	M
E	T	A	L	R	T	L	N	R	P
N	A	T	I	O	N	A	L	M	O
E	E	E	T	O	N	R	A	E	R
K	R	S	A	H	I	H	I	D	T
A	H	P	R	O	T	E	C	T	A
F	T	C	Y	B	E	R	O	E	N
G	N	I	P	P	O	H	S	P	T

Credits

The puzzles and stories in this book were created by the staff of GCHQ in their spare time.

Puzzle editor: Colin

Deputy puzzle editor: Chris

Puzzling team: Adam, Amy, Andrew, Andrew 2, Andrew 3, Andy, Andy 2, Ben, Bernie, Binod, Ceri, Chris, Chris 2, Colin, Daniel, Duncan, Elizabeth, George, Georgina, Hannah, Hannah 2, Hilary, Hollie, Ian, Jack, Jack 2, James, Jamie, Jen, Joanna, Jon, Jono, Julian, Kirsty, Lisa, Louise, Matthew, Mike, Narmin, Nickie, Noah, Peggy, Penelope, Rachel, Richard, Richard 2, Rose, Sam, Sam 2, Samuel, Sandeep, Shirley, Stephen, Steve, Thomas, Tom 2, Tom 3, Tracey, Will, Will 2, Zoe.

Chapter hosts: Colin, Elizabeth, Greg, Meg, Riley, Rose, Sandeep, Shanti.

Historical facts: Dr David Abrutat

Particular thanks go to Tom, and also to Gavin, Danni, Emily, Fiona, George 2, Hannah 3, James 2, James 3, Josh, Lucy, Nicky and Wayne.

Thanks also to the PFD agency, and the brilliant team at Penguin: Tom Rawlinson, Pippa Shaw, James Evans, Jane Tait, Sarah Connelly, Jamie Taylor, Alice Todd and the team at Dynamo.

Expert Puzzle Testers

Adam, Archie, Coco, Dulcie, Florence, Grace, Hannah, Isla, Ralph, Sophia, Thomas, William, Zayne.